UP THE RHINE AND DOWN THE DANUBE

By

DEREK R. BROWN

Published by

MELROSE BOOKS

An Imprint of Melrose Press Limited
St Thomas Place, Ely
Cambridgeshire
CB7 4GG, UK
www.melrosebooks.com

FIRST EDITION

Cover designed by Catherine McIntyre

ISBN 978-1-906561-57-4

Printed and bound in Great Britain by:
CPI Antony Rowe. Chippenham, Wiltshire

INTRODUCTION

It is interesting to recall that the eastern edge of the Roman Empire was bordered by the rivers Rhine and Danube.

The Romans built fortifications in the form of ramparts intended to mark the frontier. They were known as Limes or the Limes Romanus and our route up the Rhine and down the Danube effectively took us along the path of the Limes and the very edge of the Roman Empire.

This is an account of a voyage I made by boat along this route from Holland to Turkey, taking in the Rivers Ems, Rhine, Main, Danube and the Black Sea to finally arrive at Istanbul.

The journey of 3750 kilometres through 94 locks was spread over a period of two and half years, although the total actual travelling time was only 67 days.

The voyage started shortly after the cessation of the Bosnian war, the result of which had been to block the River Danube to navigation, which required an extended stopover in Budapest en route.

Unexpected hazards included experiencing fog on the River Rhine, and bureaucrats in Bulgaria and Romania added to the normal navigational perils.

For anybody contemplating taking this route themselves I hope they might find some useful information in the book, but for others I hope you will find it an interesting read.

The admission of Bulgaria and Romania into the EU will have the result of removing a great deal of the administrative problems I encountered. As a result I envisage that the journey I engaged on is likely to be considered as a route to be taken with less trepidation. Having removed the most difficult and frustrating experiences, the voyage could be much more relaxing. In time I feel sure that more facilities will be made available for rivercraft and anybody contemplating it should have no anxieties about taking this route. There is no better way of seeing the most varied and interesting places we passed through.

Whichever way you travel – BON VOYAGE!

INDEX

PART 1

PART 2

APPENDICES:

PART 1

CHAPTER 1

PREPARATIONS

IT HAD BEEN a long time coming, but at long last the day of departure was imminent. My interest in boats had existed for some time, ever since I picnicked on the bank of the Canal du Midi in France back in 1985 and promised myself that one day I would cruise that canal. Very soon after that I moved to live on the banks of the River Dee in Chester and acquired my first boat, and since then I have covered a great deal of the inland waterways of Europe.

My involvement with this boat had started some five years back when I visited the Amsterdam Boat Show and a particular boat appealed to me. As the boat-builder subsequently told me, he had observed that I had walked by the boat a great number of times before I eventually stepped aboard. This must have indicated that I was, as one might say, smitten by the boat.

Well the result of those few steps was now coming into effect. A year had been taken up discussing variations to the design and the layout of the accommodation and the specifications with regard to engine sizes, fuel and water tank capacities etc. The construction contract had taken time to agree, as also the part-exchange value for my existing boat, which so happened at that time to be in the south-west corner of France. The construction itself had taken two years and I subsequently decided it should remain in the locality of the boat-builder in Sneek, Holland, so that we could easily effect further modifications and additions arising from the testing of the boat. Not forgetting also that I was still carrying on a full time career in England and all this required numerous visits to Holland.

At long last all these matters had been resolved; the boat-builder's patience had been stretched to the limit. I had paid to berth the boat at his yard since the commissioning had been completed and I had enjoyed the many trips to this part of Holland, namely Friesland, in the very north, where the winter is extremely cold. It was now nice to be setting off for what would be a warmer climate.

This day it was extremely warm; although it was the beginning of September the whole of northern Europe was enjoying good weather after a very wet and disappointing August.

We were planning to be on board for a month and whereas there would be opportunities to replenish our stores there was the need for a very big shopping expedition to stock up with supplies.

Having filled the car to capacity and before returning to the boat to store everything away, I treated myself to the delightful European pastime of sitting at a pavement café. The last opportunity to indulge in having a piece of that wonderful dutch apple pie with plenty of cream. The last minute organisation of the boat in preparation for a long trip took sometime but the day for departure had arrived. I had driven to the station to collect Anto, my crew member, or First Officer as I like to consider him. He had spent the previous few days meeting up with old friends whilst in Holland. We set about filling up with diesel fuel. The cost to fill to full capacity amounted to over £300 – 500 litres in the main tank and 100 litres in the reserve tank. It had been one of our bright ideas to utilise the void space in the bathing platform at the stern of the boat to make a reserve fuel tank. We were then away in glorious sunshine with the entire work force of the boat-builders, Brandsma Jachten, to wave us off.

The first day's journey was to Bergum, a distance of three and half hours and a place we had visited previously on one of our test runs, so it was very straightforward. We knew what to expect on arrival and we were soon enjoying our evening meal and drinks on deck. It was an easy first day with no locks but plenty of traffic coming in the opposite direction.

CHAPTER 2

SNEEK TO DELFZIJL

SNEEK TO DELFZIJL in the north of Holland at the mouth of the river Ems is only a distance of about 100 kms and not particularly scenic, but Delfzijl was a good location to lock out into the North Sea and then to enter Germany via the river Ems. It was to Delftzijl we had to go first on our journey to the Black Sea, namely north instead of south

We had crossed Sneekermeer and followed the Princess Margaret canal through Croun and round Wartena and not had to use any locks. On our second day, we did not set off until 10.00; it was sunny and dry, and at times a little overcast but still very warm.

We crossed over Bergumeer, passed through Schuilenburg and came to our first lock at Gerkesklooster. It created no problems – we went in with two other similar sized vessels as well as two big commercial barges. I reflected on the first lock I had experienced in Holland, as a complete novice in Utrecht, and the problems we had encountered then, but a lot of water had gone under the bridges since and some thousands of locks later we knew what to do.

We were out of the lock by 12.30, with a sandwich lunch on the hoof and in the company of the other two similar sized vessels, one a hire boat and one clearly an experienced hand.

Initially we had been in the habit of overtaking the experienced boat but he always caught us up again when we had to wait for the many bridges to open.

They always just happened to open as he arrived and he went gaily through and we had to fall in behind him, having been hovering around waiting. The penny eventually dropped and we realised he was using his VHF to radio ahead requesting a bridge opening. We realised it was more sensible therefore to stay behind him and be able to follow through without any problems.

However on one occasion when we were dawdling and not close up to him, we nearly 'missed the boat' as the bridge was closing before we got there. Thereafter we kept close on his tail. Although he was travelling quite slowly it was clearly to our advantage to travel in convoy with him.

We came to our second lock at Groningen and had a long wait whilst one big commercial barge came down and one went up with no room in the lock for anybody else.

Immediately after leaving the lock we turned into the Elms canal; waiting at the lock gave us the opportunity to talk with the people in the other boat who it turned out were also making for Delfzijl; this again proved the wisdom of following them.

The approach into the harbour marina at Delfzijl necessitated taking a side canal and passing through two swing bridges, the second of which indicated we would have a half-hour wait. We were just about to go for a short stroll when the other waiting boats started to move out, the bridge was opening, the keeper had returned early. The harbour marina proved quite large. We were singled to a pleasant and most suitable spot on the end for mooring. When secured and before reporting to the Haven Master's office to pay our dues we called on our travelling companions to thank them with a bottle of wine for being our chaperon.

We spent a quiet evening on board after a longer and more tiring day and reflected on the fact we would soon be out of Holland.

However we opted to stay put the next day; it was very sunny and it gave us the opportunity to shop for the items we had overlooked, also to locate the Customs Office. We were going out of the EU into the North Sea, albeit for only a short time. Delfzijl was a nice typical Dutch town, nothing brilliant but interesting and we found a pleasant restaurant for our last meal in Holland.

There was quite a mist the next day, no wind, and we set off at 09.15 back down the small leg we had used to come into the marina. Through the two swing bridges back into the main canal, we cleared through customs without any problem. Together with a small German boat we went through the lock, which took us into the tidal waters of the river Ems. I had great anxieties about the customs clearance because it was essential to our plan to leave the EU and have our papers stamped accordingly and then to re-enter.

As is usually the case, if you worry about something it does not happen and if you don't it does. Things had gone according to plan and we had obtained the necessary clearance

CHAPTER 3

THE RIVER EMS

– EMDEN TO DÜSSELDORF

AFTER A SHORT trip out into the sea we came back into the river and moored along with many large boats at the Emden Yacht Club.

The following day we set off slightly earlier at 08.15, knowing we had more locks to pass through that day. We were running with the tide, which had just turned. The river narrowed after we passed Papenburg and there was not a lot of water under the boat, since the tide was only just coming in. We came upon a commercial boat and recognised the benefit of following it so as to be aware of the channel. When we arrived at the first lock we realised our inadequacy in not being able to speak German and had a two-hour delay.

We were required to wait until there was room for us with the heavy commercial traffic.

Once through the lock we appreciated the fact that the waters were no longer tidal and we passed through the next three locks without experiencing any delays. We arrived at Haren at 18.15 having taken ten hours, quite a long day.

We had been advised of a small yacht haven here which would

hopefully provide us with a suitable berth. As we rounded a bend there was the entrance to a large basin, just where we expected it to be. Most of it was taken up with large commercial vessels, but tucked away in one corner was a small boat club. It was clearly big enough to take us since it contained, in addition to a lot of small boats, one or two of similar size to ourselves. Most of all there was what one wants to see on such occasions – a human being, somebody to speak to about our berthing.

It is not wise to just tie up and hope it will be all right; one might have to if the devil drives you and there is no choice, but it is much better to first get clearance and know that the Haven Master has made you welcome. That was the position on this occasion. There was just one space available and it was just big enough. A very narrow gap to negotiate between other boats, with only inches to spare, which at the end of a long day was a pain.

However it was good to know we had a safe place for the night and the opportunity to relax and enjoy the evening.

Once secure we were given keys to the gate and told of the facilities available, the directions to the nearest shops and a restaurant and the procedures for leaving the following day.

We fortunately had a good night's sleep because the next day was to prove a long one. We eased out of our safe mooring at 09.00 and set off for the first lock. As we approached we noticed two large barges waiting to go through and took our place along with another pleasure boat waiting to be called forward. We expected this not to be too long but it proved not to be the case. Endless barges continued to arrive and the lock was of a size which just took two of them with not an inch of room left.

We had allowed plenty of time, we thought, but it was Sunday and the lock closed at one o'clock.

Well luck was on our side and along with the other pleasure boat we were just able to squeeze into the lock on the last operation before it closed for the day. We were more than relieved not to find ourselves having to spend the night moored at a lock staging, which would not have enabled us to go ashore. We had no further delays at the remaining locks but the hold-up at Munster meant that we did not get as far as we had intended and at 18.30 we felt it was time to call it a day. We had no alternative but to tie up at the canal side and hope we were not occupying a commercial barge's normal stopping place.

Although it was free there was of course no mains electrical supply, but fortunately we had our own generator for such situations. We were undisturbed except for the wash from the passing commercial barges.

Another hot sunny day took us to Herichenburg and a very warm welcome. We had arrived at 16.00, a perfect time to have a cup of tea and make a quick reconnaissance of the locality to see what was available by way of restaurants etc.

On the advice of the friendly Haven Master we opted for a German-Greek restaurant called 'Papa Christos'. The combination of the two cuisines proved interesting and it was inexpensive, a nice experience.

The boat club was situated at the junction of two canals where once there had been an interesting and ingenious engineering feature for traffic to move from one canal to the other. This was no longer in use but had been preserved as a museum piece and was a site of historical interest.

It was now not far for us to complete the journey to the Rhine and we were a little uncertain what to expect. We felt it might be wise to stop just short of having to enter the mighty river. The people in the neighbouring boat at the boat club spoke of a friend who had a ship building yard and they were sure that they would make us welcome but we were not certain that this was likely to provide what we wanted.

Whilst passing through one of the locks a local yachtsman explained that if we turned downriver on arrival at the Rhine, after the third inlet on our starboard side just after going under a bridge, there would be an ideal inlet with a suitable yacht haven and we would not have to cross over to the other side of the river.

We followed his instructions and arrived at the perfect place for us to rest and raise the necessary courage to face the grand River Rhine, with all the difficulties of big, fast-moving ships and a strong current against us.

CHAPTER 4

THE RIVER RHINE – DUISBURG TO MAIN

THE RIVER RHINE, to inland waterway boat enthusiasts, is like Mount Eiger is to mountain climbers; the peak of achievement, their ultimate goal which beforehand is viewed with trepidation.

Like everybody else, I had read books describing the heavy concentration of traffic, creating metre-high waves, likened to the M1 in England for boats. We had arrived on the Rhine at Duisburg where it joins the River Ems. We had rested at the boat haven of the Ruhrorter YC, superbly situated in an inlet close to the city's exhibition area.

We had replenished our supplies and enjoyed the facilities provided at the clubhouse, particularly the good food in their restaurant. This had a superb panoramic view of the Rhine. Sitting there watching the big ships passing up and down in a continuous stream at what seemed incredibly fast speeds had the effect of increasing our anxiety about taking the boat out into the river.

The comforts of the clubhouse were a temptation to delay our start, which was intensified by the anxiety we felt about this part of the voyage. Would we have sufficient power to make headway against the strong current? Should we be taking on a river pilot? All these anxieties were very much to the forefront of our minds.

This was made worse by the fact that we were berthed alongside a very badly damaged boat still awaiting the insurance assessors. The damage had been caused by the bow wave of a ship passing too close.

Duisburg is the biggest inland port in the world and we had been given the contact name of a ship builder on whom we paid a visit. We received a most interesting tour of his shipyard, but most important of all he gave us two complimentary tickets to a trade fair in Duisburg. Although this was for big ships, we were able to buy detailed route charts of the Rhine, something we had not been able to procure in England. So at least we now felt equipped to embark on this most challenging section of our voyage. Another purchase at the trade fair was an extending boathook, which was to prove subsequently to be one of our greatest assets.

The day of our planned start dawned to find what we assumed was an early morning mist. We delayed our start to allow time for this to clear and set off at 09.30. This was to be our first mistake. The one thing that the books had not mentioned was fog. The strength of the current was not the problem as we had feared, but what we had assumed to be mist which would clear as the day wore on, turned out to be fog, and thick fog at that. Whereas we had a very well fitted-out ship with all the appropriate equipment the one thing we did not have was radar, since for daytime travel on inland waterways we had assumed this would not be required.

It was not long before it became obvious that it was dangerous to continue, but as with all rivers, unlike canals, it is not possible to moor up just anywhere. One needs a suitable harbour and each day the voyage has to be planned with this in mind. To know just how far one can travel in a day is dependent upon availability of harbours. One plans where one is stopping each night and the journey is much like a game of leapfrog.

People have often referred to the fact that I appear to have a charmed life, in that things have gone well for me. Well today God was watching over us. To have anchored would not have been a good idea since a small ship like ours might not have been visible to one of the big vessels continuing to plough on at full speed, and going back was just as bad as going on.

Out of the fog we spotted a Dutch barge – quite large but obviously not of a size to have radar – who had decided to anchor and stay put until the fog cleared. He was big enough to be seen. The question now was how to make contact, to see if we could tie up alongside, which in itself was going to be difficult; a very dangerous manoeuvre in the fast-flowing river.

As I have said, it was a Dutch boat and of course my assistant Anto was Dutch – lucky again, you may say, but no amount of calling up on the VHF radio in Dutch, or any other language for that matter, could raise a response. Eventually contact was made and the captain came on deck to help secure a line. A very large fender positioned close to the stern and the strong rope at the front of sufficient length so that the current kept the boats apart removed the risk of the boats smashing against each other.

We stayed like that for some time, completely enveloped in fog but feeling safe. Eventually the fog cleared sufficiently for the Dutch captain to decide it was safe enough for him to continue. This now of course forced us to cast off from the safety of our mother ship, another difficult manoeuvre in such a strong current. It again required considerable skill to avoid our swinging round and smashing into the barge. By keeping the bow rope in place until the power of the engines could ensure that the boat would not be swung broadside we could then release it and move forward. We were making for a safe haven at 749 on the river just outside Düsseldorf, but we were only half the distance we had hoped to travel on our first day on the Rhine. After what we had experienced and the danger of the fog coming down again it would have been foolish not to take advantage of a yacht club in a small inlet at 762. Life is not that easy, and apart from the difficulties of turning off the river, the problem of getting into the haven was made worse because there was a barge in the entrance fixing a cable.

It was not clear which side we should pass the vessel. Getting it wrong and getting caught up with the cable would have had disastrous results. Usually the workboats indicate which side it is safe to pass on by showing a red and white sign on the safe side and a plain red one on the danger side, but not this boat. We eventually received not clear but perhaps comforting hand signals to confirm on which side to pass.

The leapfrogging system from haven to haven is fine as long as there is 'room at the inn'. Most places are full with permanent residents and there is not sufficient demand from pleasure craft on the Rhine to justify them keeping a place available for casual visitors. They could charge a higher rate but the demand is not sufficient.

Perhaps this may change, but the recent introduction of the rule that boats over a certain length must take on board a pilot on the River Rhine will make it less likely.

Well, God was still looking after us and there was a superb place at the entrance to the haven, which was sufficiently large to accommodate us and very easily accessible. After a difficult day this was of great benefit, since having to manoeuvre into a tight mooring when tired can be very difficult. Apparently the boat which normally occupied this space had been taken by the owners on a trip to Venice and it was not known when they would be returning, so we could tie up and relax – or so we thought. Once we had made the boat fully secure our luck changed when a large boat of similar size as ourselves arrived and we were congratulating ourselves for having arrived first when the penny dropped and we realised that this was the boat returning from Venice and we were in their place.

They were delightful people and provided we moved out they were quite happy for us to moor up alongside them as long as we were well fended, which was fine for us, and we were well positioned to leave the next morning.

The next day dawned with no sign of fog or mist. In fact it was a fine day with a clear blue sky. We set off feeling a lot more confident than the previous day, only to encounter a problem very quickly. As it has to be expected with the strong river-flow, sandbanks are built up at the entrance to inlets where such harbours are constructed. Well, coming out into the river at a careful speed we managed to get the boat very firmly stuck on the top of the sandbank. Despite powerful engines, we could not move until, with the help of the large waves created by two large tankers passing by together, we managed to ride ourselves clear.

We soon caught on to the blue-flagging procedure where ships cross to the opposite side of the river and pass starboard to starboard instead of port to port. We felt it wise to follow suit, but it involved crossing over the centre of the river where the current flow is much stronger compared with nearer the bank. We made good time and at 16.00 reached Köln and tided up in an excellent haven very central to the city. The only problem was to watch the height of the footbridge across the entrance and the numerous cruise ships tied up alongside the town quay. We reversed into the space allotted with only inches on either side. After six hours at the wheel this can be a difficult task. By 16.30 we were tied up, changed and out in the city after paying the most efficient harbour master the appropriate dock dues and being presented with a very useful bag, which we are still using. Köln is a fine city, particularly round the most famous and magnificent cathedral, which was of course essential for us to visit. A meal at a nearby restaurant was a rewarding experience. The atmosphere and food were truly traditionally Germanic – the waiter's dress, the benches, the wooden tables and the décor looked as if they had not changed for 100 years.

We took advantage the next day of the excellent facilities at the haven to fill up with diesel, and we left at 09.30, arriving at Neuwied just north of Koblenz at 18.30. A good stopping place in a big lagoon, the entrance to which is not obvious because you cannot see the boats until you round a corner after turning into the entrance, and there is no sign on the river. Fortunately there were some rowers who, when we enquired from them about the haven, led us slowly into this most welcome retreat off the river. After such a straightforward day we had come to the conclusion that all these reports about strong currents and waves were old wives' tales, but this impression was soon to be dispelled.

We left Niewed at 09.30 and after three or four hours of easy going in the wake of a Dutch barge called *Ranamara*, whom we had adopted as our pilot boat, things changed. Yes, we had read that this section near Bingen lock and St Goar was tricky but could not have visualised the experience we were to encounter.

For half an hour it was like experiencing white-water rafting. We felt we owed a deep debt of gratitude to our pilot ship who showed us the way and onto whose tail we clung as we passed through these treacherous waters with the sight of jagged rocks sticking out of the water only yards from the well-buoyed channel. It certainly helped to concentrate the mind. We arrived at Bingen at our scheduled stopping time of 17.30. It was a most welcoming haven and provided first-class facilities, including an excellent restaurant. We were too late for the shops but still took a relaxing walk into the town.

The next day we felt the need to relax a little and took our time to replenish the water tanks and tidy the boat. The distance still to cover to Main was only 30 km and would not take too long.

Mr Barry Sheffield's book, *Inland Waterways of Germany*, which appears to be the only available source of information on German waterways, was our bible, and listed three or four yacht havens at Main, so hopefully we should have no problem in finding a berth and had no reason to worry. We came to realise that the German waterways are well equipped to deal with the big commercial vessels and also pleasure craft up to, say, eight metres with a draft of no more than a metre. We exceeded these dimensions by a fair margin and fell between the two stools. We were to find that whereas there appears to be a good supply of boat havens when reading Mr Sheffield's book, you eventually come to realise that it was pitched at the smaller vessels.

At Main the depth of the inlet proved to be only just 1.5 metres, and we inched our way in, feeling the bottom often. In the centre of the four clubs was a small repair yard, the owner of which was most helpful but had no direct involvement with any of the four private clubs and could not help, except to suggest we take pot luck and berth the boat at one of the vacant stages.

It was Sunday and we had met a lot of pleasure craft out on

the river – mostly speedy types who for no apparent reason like to show off. So it was no surprise that there were a number of vacant places, the owners clearly out for the day. It was essential to keep our props in the deepest part and we tied up bow first. When safely secured we felt we deserved a break and took a short walk in the centre. After visiting a chocolate factory and enjoying tea and cakes we returned to the boat to find, as you may have guessed, two irate guys waiting for us, to say that we had taken their place. This needed an apology, which was received with ill grace, but the boatyard owner came to our aid and allowed us to tie up alongside his workshop.

CHAPTER 5

RIVER MAIN AND THE MAIN DANUBE CANAL – MAIN TO REGENSBURG

On Monday 20 September we woke to realise that our journey along the Rhine had been completed without any mishap and that boating, at least for a time, should be back to normal. We were feeling more relaxed because we would not need to concern ourselves about stopping places since surely there should be sufficient. Anto went off to shop whilst I did the necessary servicing of the engines, cleaning water filters and topping up the engine oil etc. I was also able to get an engineer to check out the steering, which I noticed was squeaking a little. He assured me that everything was fine. Eventually Anto returned fully laden on our folding bicycle and after storing everything away we set off at midday without getting stuck on the bottom, to our relief. We had to cross the Rhine to the other side where the Main joined it and immediately noticed the difference; virtually no current. Whereas the locks were quite large the rise was only between three and three and a half metres and the journey went smoothly with little waiting time. At each lock it was necessary to report, with documents to be checked. After three locks we came to Frankfurt, which looks like Manhattan. With no facilities to tie up, we carried on, being careful to observe the speed limit, which is strictly controlled. A further two locks on, we identified what appeared to be an ideal mooring place and, encouraged by a man and girl standing on a boat moored alongside a clubhouse to tie up alongside another boat, we thought our luck was in. Having secured the boat firmly, and delighted to see electrical points so that we could have mains electricity without resorting to our generator, we were asked to come to the clubhouse. Here we were introduced to a German woman who by saying the words "please wait a minute" gave us the feeling that there might be a problem. These words were the limit of her English. After a good half-hour of their frenzied activity on the telephone, and with Anto speaking to her in Dutch, it became apparent that she was concerned. The weight of our boat tied to the other steel boat, and the waves from passing ships, might damage the repair work which was being done to the quay.

Well, time had gone on and we had waited more than an hour; it was getting late and dark, where could we go at this late hour? More long telephone calls were being made, with the result that she assured us she had obtained permission for us to tie up on the other side of the river at the official river authority's quay, normally prohibited to everybody except the WSD authority vessels.

The WSD – short for Wasser und Schiffahrts Direktion (water and shipping authority) – has seven regions administered by the Bundeswasserstrassen, the German waterways network. These are very extensive and exist for a practical purpose, being used extensively by commercial vessels. Although the German waterways are freely available to visitors, there are strictly imposed regulations and it is advisable to be fully acquainted with them.

By eight o'clock we were safely secure again and felt safe for the night, but realised that we would again be having problems with overnight mooring places. The many yacht havens referred to in the reference books proved to have inadequate depth for us.

We had decided to leave the next morning quite early and this proved wise since, as we were about to get under way, the manager of the WSD arrived and immediately asked what the hell we were doing there. We assured him that we had the permission of his superior but clearly he was not aware of this. Since we were leaving, he was less concerned and the situation was resolved as he waved us off, realising that we must not be tempted to use their excellent facilities without their permission in the future.

We made good progress, falling in behind two barges that entered locks together and still left enough room for us. As long as we could keep up with them it was fine. We covered the distance of 70 kilometers and six locks to Miltenberg and were able to tie up at the town quay by 15.30. This gave plenty of time to make a reconnoitre visit and still go back into the town for dinner. Miltenberg we found to be one of the most beautiful towns in Bavaria, full of character. Fortunately it was not considered sufficiently important to have been subjected to bombing in the Second World War, except for the bridge, which was blown up three weeks before the end of the war. The town has therefore been able to preserve its interesting houses dating from the sixteenth century, for which it is famous.

The city had been occupied by the Swedish army during the Thirty Years War, and prior to that the town had been very wealthy by reason of the fact that they could collect substantial taxes from the traders who passed through it.

It was the junction of the routes from Prague, Budapest and Venice in the south and Köln and Amsterdam to the north.

In the fourteenth century it had been the richest town in the Bishopric of Mainz. All this history was apparent as we walked around the cobbled streets and the market square containing a superb Renaissance fountain.

All this, with interesting shops and hotels, one of which was the oldest in Germany, made us vote Miltenberg the best town we visited during our time in Germany.

We started off well after leaving Miltenberg. Anto had first slipped back into the town to get a few things we had forgotten to buy the previous day. Again we chose to follow a fast barge and did this for the first three locks, but at the third we were forced to wait for another barge to come into the lock. On leaving we decided we should follow the second barge. This proved a bad decision because it was going much slower and the first one went racing on whilst we had to dawdle behind our chosen leader. When it decided to stop we found we had missed the earlier barge at the next lock and had to wait a very long time. Eventually they let us in. In our frustration and bearing in mind that the bollards were becoming increasingly far apart, and because I like to be fastened fore and aft, we nearly had a major catastrophe, as we raced back and forth trying to get secure before the lock gates closed and the water came rushing in. After doing another lock without incident, we regained our confidence and we were again happy that we had the right scheme with our ropes. Shortly after this lock we found an excellent quay to moor at in Lohr. Although the book said two metres of depth it seemed more like four metres. The next day was to be a long day; initially we were concerned that the generator was for some reason playing up, but everything settled down and we managed to get away by 9.30 and did well to do seven locks and 72 kilometres in nine hours to reach Ochsenfurt. Here again we found a superb town quay with our own little garden, a lovely setting near an old bridge.

It was one of the most attractive moorings we experienced. We had stopped on the way to refuel with diesel and took on 400 litres. We went into town and enjoyed a typical German meal. The next day started cloudy and we encountered rain and a thunderstorm, which can be a pain when working a lock. For some reason the lock keeper at Randersacker lock was very difficult. Leaving Ochsenfurt at 09.00 and following the same barge for six locks, we managed to cover another 62 kilometres and seven locks in seven and half hours, meaning we could tie up at 16.30, which is a perfect time to rest and have an enjoyable evening.

We moored in Schweinfurt at the end of a quay where private commercial boats loaded their passengers at 10.00 in the morning. We were concerned that we might be asked to move, but there was no problem. When we woke up, we found it raining very heavily, but realising we had a tight schedule to keep we could not be deterred from keeping going, and set off at nine with the aim to get to Bamberg, where the River Main joins the Main-Danube Canal. Despite the atrocious weather and the difficult currents from side streams and the turbulence from a double barge in front who made us slow right down, the locks were no problem and after the final four locks we arrived at Bamberg at 16.00.

But we could find nowhere to tie up that was suitable. There was a wall along a road, but nothing to secure to except some fence posts, which with the swell from passing ships would no doubt have been damaged by morning.

There was however the most perfect place, a WSA staging with their regional office nearby. Necessity must, but I was reluctant to stay there without permission. Having tied up, I eventually located somebody in the office who said that because it was Saturday night we could stay, as long as we were away by 09.00 on Monday morning. This was brilliant news – we needed a day's rest, and what better day than Sunday? Although it proved to be a wet and miserable day, in the evening there was a beautiful sunset. Initially we spent the time cleaning up and tidying the boat and then took a short walk into the centre and found a most enchanting place.

Bamberg has been granted the status of a world heritate site by Unesco. We enjoyed the charm of the town, with a skyline of many church steeples rising above a multitude of gables on steep tiled or blue slate roofs. Fortunately this town was also not damaged during the Second World War, and we were lucky to have a whole day to explore it. The River Regnitz, which is a tributary to the Main, runs through the town, and the most decorative of buildings, the Town Hall, strides the river and provides a unique setting. The Dom was another building not to be missed, where we were given a most interesting conducted tour. In this old imperial and episcopal city first mentioned in 902 AD, the area comprising a maze of narrow alleys with old fishermen's houses is aptly called Bamberg's Little Venice.

The town itself was some distance from where we had moored the boat, but it was an essential visit since it was a place not to be missed. After our day of rest we were ready to recommence the voyage, and bearing in mind the conditions relating to our mooring, we made sure we were away by 08.50. It transpired that our day of rest had been essential, since until now the locks by comparison had been child's play.

The Main-Danube canal has to rise 800 feet to the summit, and to achieve this, the locks have to be deep. Three of them rise over 25 feet, with no floating bollards to which one could hook on, and they float up the side of the lock as the water rises in the lock. Instead one has to manually move up the ropes, on hooks in the side of the lock, like a game of leapfrog but vertical.

Twelve hundred years ago, Charlemagne, Emperor of the Holy Roman Empire, ordered a canal to be dug between the rivers Main and Danube. The difficulties of digging a 100-mile trench through the mountains of central Europe proved too difficult even for the Romans.

However, the plan was resurrected in 1921 but it was not until about 70 years later that the Main-Danube canal finally opened.

It is 171 kilometres long and completes the missing link to make navigation possible between the North Sea and the Black Sea, a distance of 3,500 kilometres and the journey we were undertaking. At the highest point it is 406 metres above sea level.

We set off from Bamberg with a certain amount of anxiety because of the height of the locks and the fact that there would be no floating bollards. We knew it was going to be difficult with only the two of us. The first lock was designed as if one were entering into a tunnel and we waited outside the mammoth door-like gate at the end of a funnel. When it opened it was like going into the mouth of a whale or into a vast empty tomb with walls towering high on both sides. This lock was only 10.9 metres high; compared with some of the later ones, which would be over two and a half times as high at 25 metres, it was not difficult. We completed this lock with a feeling of satisfaction, but had five more to do that day before we reached Nürnberg, and the last two were 18.3 metres in height. Remembering what I said earlier, that there were no floating bollards on these locks, and the need for speed to tie up both front and aft before the lock keeper closed the gate behind us and started letting in the water, and then to keep moving the ropes up as the water rose, and keeping the boat hard against the lock side, meant that by the time we got to Nürnberg we were shattered. In the last lock of the day, at Kriegenbrunn, we were nearly in tears and wondered how we were going to be able to carry on at this pace. When we eventually arrived at Nürnberg we were able to moor in a haven and relax. Tied up on a good quay just past the town, and despite all the hard work, we went to shop for fresh bread and milk in the knowledge that the worst was over. The next day we set off at 07.30. It was raining very heavily. Hoping things could only get better, since we were aware that after the first lock, which was only 9.4 metres by comparison to the last three locks the previous day, this would be easy, and it had floating bollards on the left side of the lock. As long as we could get positioned by these, life would be so much easier, and then, after the summit, we would be going down.

It had been our intention to tie up at the summit, where we understood there was a good quay, but when we got there at about two o'clock this was not the case. There were no bollards to secure to. Fortunately we had time to continue, in the hope of finding something better. After the next lock there was a yacht club at 120, but this proved not to be suitable either. The wife of a Dutch barge owner with whom Anto had a shouted conversation in the lock encouraged us by telling us that there was an ideal haven further on and that they would show us the place. We therefore continued on and through another lock, but when we emerged it was beginning to get dark, and driving at night was not our plan, and how were we going to know when we had reached this ideal mooring place?

We were still following the Dutch barge and suddenly they started to shine their searchlight onto the right bank, and we realised that this was the signal to us for the haven. We just made out the very small entrance, and with the aid of our own strong searchlight, managed to turn in to find a large landing stage and a clubhouse set back from it. By letting our light shine periodically onto the windows, giving the impression of it being unintentional, we caught a guy's attention. He came down and helped us tie up. When secure, we went into the clubhouse and enjoyed a much-needed meal and went to bed relieved that we had a safe place. We felt sufficiently relaxed to delay our start until midday. We were aware that it was all downhill from here. Our plan was to get to Budapest, where we could leave the boat for the winter and had already made arrangements with a very conveniently situated marina in what had once been the Budapest Ship Yard. They would be taking the boat out of the water to winterise it. However, we had taken slightly more than three weeks to get this far and it was now the end of September. The weather was turning cold and we had about 750 kilometres still to go to Budapest.

We had allowed only four weeks for the whole trip and I had promised to be back in England for around 10 October.

We set off to go through the last three locks of the canal before it joined the Danube at Keilham. All the locks were easy – just fasten onto floating bollards at the top, the water level just slowly fell and it was no effort. Unhook and drive out, a piece of cake by comparison to what we had been used to.

It is not easy to see where canals join rivers; they seem to merge into each other, but we soon realised we had entered the Danube when we felt the strong current. It was a great shock. Our first exposure to this fast-flowing river, to which we had to adjust from the canal, was made more difficult because we were confronted by an enormous luxury yacht 70 metres long, coming towards us at over 30 knots and suddenly stopping. We later found out that it was undergoing trials from the famous shipyard of PR Marine, situated here on the Danube.

We held back so as not to interfere with the manoeuvres; we were buffeted by the considerable turbulence it caused but we still refrained from overtaking. We then noticed that it had turned into a large harbour with a narrow slanting entrance into the river. We recognised that this might be a good stopping place, but to get into the narrow opening was going to be a difficult task. First of all we had to go downstream, turn and come back upstream against the strong current, then point the boat to turn after the opening so that the current would bring us back to the opening just at the right time to give strong power to get out of the current and then to instantly reduce the engine power the minute we were in the entrance channel. To our delight we found a large shipyard with numerous boats, and immediately went to tie up at one of the stages. A very pleasant man came to us, and when we explained that we wished to moor for the night he took us to the other side of the haven, which was for visitors.

We made secure and went to find the office, which not only comprised the office but a marina and an Italian restaurant on the top floor.

Nobody could speak English very well, with the exception of the accountant, and with his help we were able to establish that this was a big ship builder and repairer and had facilities to house boats indoors over the winter. Well, you can imagine how our minds began to think. We had no need to go on to Budapest – we could leave the boat here for the winter, and in fact it would be better because it would be indoors and undercover.

We established the cost for the wintering package and agreed that we would leave the boat with them. We would close down, pack up and arrange to go back to England the next day. They made only one request – that we empty the boat of the sewage water etc. in the river and not in the haven. When they took the boat out of the water they did not want to create a dirty mess in their boathouse. This necessitated us having to go out into the river to do the business, as you may say, and complete again the difficult manoeuvre of getting back into the haven through the narrow entrance without being washed against the rocks in the entrance. We completed it without mishap and rewarded ourselves with a magnificent meal in the Italian restaurant where to this day we consider we had the finest minestrone soup we have ever tasted. This may or may not have been the best, but the feeling of elation, realising we were free for a time of our responsibilities, made anything we were given to eat taste fantastic, and the Italian wine provided the extra enjoyment to what was our farewell party for a time.

CHAPTER 6

RIVER DANUBE – REGENSBURG TO VIENNA

THE WINTER IS over and the time has come for us to recommence our voyage. We had felt confident about leaving the boat in such safe hands at PR Marine at Sall On Danau, the famous boat-building company owned by Herr Heinrich Beibner, and had no doubt that the boat would be ready and waiting for us.

We had planned our visit, having ensured that we would have plenty of time to complete the remainder of the journey to Budapest without undue pressure. We had organised our other commitments to free ourselves from the need to return. The time was the last week of April and we hoped that the melting snow combined with the very heavy rain had not turned the Danube into the fast-flowing river it can become in springtime.

Our plan was to travel back to the boat by flying from Manchester to Vienna and to take the train north to Regensburg. This way we could take a train back to Vienna from Budapest for our return flight. Vienna Airport is blessed with an excellent bus transfer service from the airport to the railway station, taxis being extremely expensive in Vienna. Not that this worked out as planned. On the way out our flight was delayed to an extent that to wait for the bus would have meant we would not catch the train, and a very expensive taxi had to be used. We planned to spend the night in Regensburg before going onto the boat, the reason being that we would arrive in the morning and have a free day to make the boat safe and comfortable for the first night aboard.

It is very much like moving into a new house when a boat has been laid up for the winter. Regensburg is a delightful place to stay, as is all of the Bavarian area of Germany. We secured the best room in the hotel at which we had made our reservation and our initial sortie found a delightful restaurant in what we would describe as a church cloister.

Our amble before dinner obviously took us to inspect the river on which we were about to travel, and what better place to see it but from the town bridge. This comprised a number of small arches through which the water was rushing at such speed that it created different levels on each side of the bridge.

A most picturesque site, but whereas I judged that the arches were just wide enough to take our boat, to navigate through such a fast-flowing aperture would be suicidal, and yet bigger boats were moored on either side. There was something wrong – there were no navigation signs on the arches (indicating priority for up and down vessels etc.). On reflection I realised there must be another way.

The following morning, before setting off to join the boat we made further enquiries, to be told that there was a bypass canal to the town with a lock. This had to be seen since it is of significant benefit if one has knowledge of the lock before approaching by water. The lock was big but not a problem, and there were plenty of mooring places on either side, so we returned to the hotel to collect our luggage and set off to see our boat again.

During the journey by taxi we set up a conversation with the driver and explained that we wished to be taken to PR Marine in

Soll on Danau. He expressed surprise, which was not as great as our surprise when he told us that they had gone bankrupt. Well, what about our boat – looking after it and preparing it again for use after winterisation? He was adamant they had gone down. Well, he was right, they had, but the servicing and storing business was operated by a separate company from the boat building and this was still trading. Our boat was safe and in place, looking pleased to see us, if a boat can express itself.

Alberto the engineer had done his work well and the only casualty of the winter had been one battery, which was quickly replaced, and everything was in working order. It did not take long to get the boat shipshape and filled with fuel and water. A trip into the town for provisions was marred by wet and windy weather but it was good to feel we were stocked up and ready to be off again. The next morning we needed to make a visit into the town before we set off, to get cash since it is not wise just to rely on credit cards. My bank had stopped the use of Eurocheques, which had always been an easy and safe way to get money. Eventually we were able to find a hole-in-the-wall machine to dispense the much-needed currency. We eventually got under way and the first lock presented no problem.

At the second we had to moor up and wait. There was a speaker system to communicate with the lock keeper on the quay side. This was fine and we managed to make contact with him but could not understand a word he said in German. We managed to get a passer-by who also spoke English to speak to him for us and to interpret which only amounted to "wait there until I call you in". The waiting was not long before a big ship arrived and we were called up over the loudspeaker to enter the lock after the ship. There was just sufficient room.

We followed the ship to the next lock and were similarly commanded to come in behind this ship. This was the Regensburg lock we had visited, so we tied up immediately after the lock where we had seen other boats moored the previous day. We were then able to walk into Regensburg again and have a lovely meal at the same restaurant we had visited previously and enjoyed so much. Having enjoyed our time in Regensburg, which we had come to like very much, we set off at 09.00 in cold and wet weather. As we left our quay, primarily used by big commercial barges, one was taking our place. It was fortunate that we had not gone into town to get fresh milk before we left. We locked through the first lock at 11.00 and the next at 13.00 and arrived at Deggendorf a little after 15.00. The town quay was too shallow, so we moored on the end of a commercial quay next to a Romanian barge and near the railway sidings. It seemed safe and I cycled into town for the much-needed milk. The next day was cloudy but dry and again we set off by our targeted time of 09.00. At the second lock we had to wait an hour for two boats to arrive, and we were about to follow them into the lock when the gates started to close because we were too slow. Fortunately the lock keeper relented and let us in; despite this we arrived at 13.30 at Passau and saw a convenient spot in the main quay between pleasure cruise boats. At first we tried to back into the place, then realised the futility of trying to reverse against the strong current. We did the right thing to turn around and come in against the current. Arriving early gave us the time to enjoy this very pleasant town, visit the magnificent cathedral with its famous organ and admire the many fine buildings, in addition to visiting the shops and going out for dinner at a very pleasant restaurant overlooking the quay. Our dinner was tinged with anxiety. When checking the cooling-water filters in the engine room I had noticed that the prop shafts were turning. Why was this when the engines were turned off and the boat was stationary? Had the propeller become loose or what? Although I tried to put this out of my mind over dinner it still concerned me.

On our return to the boat and before going to bed I referred to the engine manual. To my relief I found that this was normal.

We set off the next day in sunny but very windy weather. The quay we had moored to in the centre of the town was normally reserved for river cruise boats, but the police had kindly allowed us to stay there. We slowed down at the Austrian customs quay, but there was no sign of life and we proceeded on; formal barriers between EEC countries have been dispensed with except in and out of the UK. We were now in Austria and changed the courtesy flag for an easy run with only three locks to get to Linz. It looked nice – it had a harbour – but we received no co-operation from the boat club and were told 'no room at the inn'. We found a derelict commercial harbour and tied up with the hope that no one would come. We stayed on board that evening and left the next day at 06.30. We arrived at the first lock at 09.15 but did not get through until 10.45, taking one and half hours.

At Grain, I wanted to stop for sentimental reasons – namely to visit a small hotel where I had stayed many years before on my first visit to this part of the world to see what the Danube was like. We aborted our efforts to tie up after nearly going aground on a submerged quay and proceeded on. Over the next stretch there are a sequence of traffic lights. We found them difficult to understand.

We met another big boat coming through this section in the opposite direction and realised that we might be in contravention of the rules and turned back. We waited for the lights to change to another grouping, still not clear as to the meaning, and then continued with extreme caution.

We continued looking for a place to stop but none was suitable. Eventually at Yibs we went into an inlet where there was a perfect quay near a factory but nobody about to ask for permission to stay. However it was quite perfect and as long as no ship came to tie up there we were safe. The next day we had intended to leave early at 08.00, just in case anybody came, but our plans were thwarted when our starboard engine failed. We now had to find somebody. This time we tried harder and found the factory to which the quay belonged, and they telephoned for a mechanic. He came and located the fault in the starter and we eventually got away at 10.30, reaching the first lock by 11.30. No journey on the Danube could be complete without a visit to Melk Abbey. We were able to tie up to one of the new landing stages primarily for cruise ships but with little jetties at the ends for smaller boats.

It was a steep walk up to the Abbey from the small town of Melk, which was mentioned in Roman times as the 'Namare' castellum.

The Abbey is an imposing Bendectine Monastery with magnificent views over the surrounding countryside for considerable distances in all directions and looks down on the River Danube as it stretches below. It was constructed during the first half of the 18th century and houses a collection of historic books, but for me the highlight was the beautiful baroque church itself.

I had been fortunate to visit it on a previous occasion for a Christmas Eve mass. An experience I will never forget was the singing on that occasion of 'Silent Night'; it sounded so much better in German.

The other place not to be missed on this section of the Danube, a bit further on from Melk, is Dürnstein, and we were able to tie up and spend a few hours there.

This town is dominated by the ruins of Kuenrigger Castle, in which King Richard the Lion-Heart was held prisoner by Duke Leopold V. He was on his way back home from the third crusade when he was captured, and the tale goes that his minstrel Blondel walked around Dürnstein Castle singing the King's favourite song, and this managed to attract the King's attention.

After this we planned to go on to Kremms to stop for the night but again our planned stopping place was not suitable because it was too shallow. A little further on there was a large industrial haven which we gingerly entered. A large ship was being loaded with grain but we selected a quiet, unoccupied corner to tie up. I though it appropriate to seek permission and set off to find the appropriate office. After seeking directions from a number of people I eventually located the right place and the right person. I explained what we were doing and not only received his permission but the company Mierka Danaughton's emblem in the form of a flag, which we have retained to this day as a memento. This gave us the confidence for me to cycle off to the nearby village and stock up with provisions from the shops some distance away. Tonight was the first night since we had set off from Saal that we had been off the river. The fact was we were in the docks, surrounded by containers and silos, and there was a train shunting alongside, so one had to be very careful when getting off the boat onto the quay to look both ways and ensure that the train was not coming, but we were safe. Leaving the next day at 08.00, after a good night's sleep, we reached the first lock (Altenworth) at 09.30 but did not clear it until 11.00. It had a 16-metre fall.

The second one, at Greifenstein, with another fall of 14 metres, brought us to Vienna by 14.00.

We knew of a nice new marina where we had made prior arrangements to stay.

It was first necessary to report to the reception, which involved tying up at a quay on the fast-flowing river. They then directed us to a quay in the downriver section, which was very difficult to enter.

The pontoon they had allocated was not very stable but we persuaded them to allow us to tie up on a much stronger one where we were able to stay for three nights to enjoy the sights of Vienna.

A few days in Vienna were not to be missed; there were things we needed to deal with, one of which was to replenish the gas for cooking. Having a berth near a station only three stops from Stephansplatz, the very hub of Vienna, we would be able to enjoy the opportunities this fine city could provide.

Accepting that the gas requirement was a priority, we felt that this needed to be dealt with first and then we could relax. What we thought could be resolved simply did not prove quite so easy. At the design stage we had opted to have four small gas containers rather than one big one, which would have required changing less frequently but would be very heavy for moving around. Trying to get replacements often involves some distance to go and although we had invested in a small folding trolley this could still prove very hard work, so four small canisters were more practical than one large one.

A small boat showroom with repair facilities at the marina was the first obvious port of call. No, surprisingly they did not supply gas, but they did know a man who did. The only problem was that he was over the other side of town and finding him would involve taking the train and changing twice, taxis as previously mentioned being very expensive. "Will he not deliver?" I asked, but no, that was not possible; also there was quite some distance to walk from the train station.

Austria is a highly regulated society and I could not imagine that, among the long list of prohibited items which could not be taken on their very efficient metro system, would not be flammable gas containers, so they would have to be kept out of sight: two could be fitted into a holdall and zipped up. Empty they were not heavy. Carrying one holdall each, we set off, knowing that if we could bring back four full ones we would be set up for some time. It was a fair walk to the nearest station at Vorgartenstasse and it took us about an hour to complete the journey. Locating the address was not so easy and required asking for directions a number of times. It had become a very hot day and the whole exercise was becoming a pain, but as with all our problems we had to persevere and could not afford to give in; but we could not be certain that if and when we located this place, they would be able to fill our containers. Hot and exhausted, we found it and yes they could supply us, so leaving the containers with them to fill we found a nearby café to refresh ourselves. To avoid the expense of a taxi we felt confident we could make the return journey by metro with the full containers. We made certain that the containers were not visible and the holders zipped up, but they were extremely heavy and we were concerned lest we were stopped. Eventually the task was completed and we were ready to enjoy Vienna.

No visit to Vienna is complete without a trip out to Schönbrunn Palace, the former summer palace of the Imperial Family, so off we went on a beautiful sunny day. I recall my first visit on a cold winter's day just before New Year, with snow on the ground and the temperature well below freezing. Whatever the time of year the grand architecture of this building in the well laid out formal grounds creates a picture and an atmosphere of grandeur. Whether it is the name or the era, the period of history when the Hapsburgs ruled has always created a fascination for me.

A visit to the opera house was the other great must-do, but the only performance available to us required sitting through five hours of Verdi. Most important to us was the opportunity to enjoy the café society with good coffee and expensive cakes in grand 19th-century buildings; it was costly but delightful. Our favourite was in Michaeler Platz, just opposite the gates to the Hofburg Complex containing the former imperial apartments and on the route taken by the horse-drawn carriages which provide so much atmosphere in Vienna. Not far from this café we were lucky to chance upon something that proved invaluable to our voyage. Bookshops always interested me, particularly if they have a good nautical section. In Kohl Market Street was such a shop. The basement was given over to the most extensive selection of maritime books that I have ever seen. Bearing in mind Austria is not on the sea, this might appear odd. My enquiries to date about river guides to the Danube had only produced detailed river charts as far as Mohács, on the Hungarian border; thereafter there was apparently only Rod Heikell's *The Danube*, which although useful was not a chart showing the channel buoyage or suitable berthing facilities. My enquiries to the shop manager produced a series of books, eight in all, covering the entire length of the Danube. They had been produced very recently by Pierre Verberght from Belguim, and provided in detail all the information, kilometre by kilometre, with buoys and the channel markings etc. They were in a 'do-it-yourself' printed form, photographed pages secured with ring-binding and a plastic cover, but these were a tremendous find.

All the information we would need was contained in them, albeit they were in German, but that could be translated without too much difficulty. Anybody contemplating making such a trip should not consider doing it without them. If nothing else our stay in Vienna was rewarded by this find, which subsequently proved invaluable. So all in all we enjoyed our few days in Vienna.

CHAPTER 7

RIVER DANUBE – VIENNA TO BUDAPEST

HAVING ENJOYED OUR stay in Vienna and rested from the concentration required in steering the boat, we set off again, this time to get to Bratislava. We took the opportunity at the marina to fill up with diesel – we still had a good supply but it is always wise to fill up when you can; you cannot be sure of easily accessible places to take on fuel.

We left at 09.30 and cleared the new lock just outside Vienna quite quickly; two hours later we came to one of the most important points in the voyage for us. This was the border between Austria and Slovakia, which was then the border for leaving the EU. This necessitated clearing customs, and if there could ever be a stupid place to situate a customs post, this must be it.

The current runs strongest on the outside edge of a bend, and yes, this is where the pontoon was sited. With the strong current that was running, it would have been virtually impossible to stop and tie up in the direction of the river flow. We had to turn about and come back to the pontoon; the current against us on the bend was running at about ten knots. So with our engines at full power we could just very slowly get back and eventually secure ourselves to the pontoon.

It was Saturday afternoon on Easter Weekend and it would appear that they had brought out of retirement an old guy to cover this duty when no doubt the regular staff wanted to be with their families. He could speak no English, so in answer to his questions when examining the ship's papers we answered "yes" until he produced a sign of surprise or concern on his face and immediately corrected it to "no". Eventually he indicated we were free to proceed. He appeared as pleased as us that the interview was concluded, and we carefully but hurriedly cast off from this so badly located pontoon.

At least we were out of the EU, which was important for us; we now proceeded to the Slovakian customs post a little further on; it was on the opposite side of the river and less difficult to tie up. We scanned the post with our binoculars and came to the conclusion that it was deserted, so that there appeared to be little point in making all the efforts required to stop and tie up, and continued on our way.

By 13.30 we had arrived at Bratislava, the capital of Slovakia, a place I had visited once before at Christmas time. I held memories of the delightfully old Dickensian town in the grip of a cold and icy winter. Very similar to the old scenes depicted on many of our Christmas cards and so full of atmosphere. I was looking forward very much to a return visit.

It was an essential stopping place, not only for this reason but because we had not identified anywhere else to stop after this until Esztergom, which was 148 kilometres further on. There was the usual array of pontoons for the cruise ships, but we could not use these, and if we did, what would happen if in the middle of the night one arrived and we were in its place? There was a wall near a bridge and it just seemed possible that we might be able to tie up alongside.

With the strong current and the waves created by large ships passing, the swell against the wall was very strong and we very nearly had a major disaster by being smashed against it before we had the wisdom to abort our efforts to tie up. I was slowly and reluctantly coming to the conclusion, much to my disappointment, that Bratislava might prove a no-go town when I noticed slightly further on an inlet into an industrial haven. We turned with great relief into the slack water and could at least feel less pressurised.

It was full of very derelict vessels, but this was a poor country and most of them would be in use. There was no room except against a wall under a bridge, and we decided that we should at least tie up for the night here. Once we were secured I did a quick recce of the area to find it was a cement works but did not currently appear to be operating and the ground gave the impression of the moon's surface.

We had been able to find on the quay face sufficient reinforcement bars to make secure to and at least felt safe to spend the night here, but any idea of going into Bratislava and leaving the boat unattended was out of the question for security reasons, but anyway we were too far away and had no transport. The weather was not bad and we had had a tiring day, what with the customs etc., so what was wrong in having a quiet evening in this rather desolate location? After the much-welcome pot of tea and a rest, Anto was just starting to prepare the evening meal when he asked what was this official looking boat with two men in uniform doing coming toward us? I thought he was joking but soon realised he was not; very soon they were alongside and had boarded our boat. Of course they had no command of the English language. But as Slovakian customs officials, why would they need to?

One does not need to understand Slovakian to realise the first demand would be 'Let us see your papers' and the second, 'Why were your passports not stamped when you entered the country?' After much effort we managed to get them to understand that there had been nobody at the customs post. They accepted this with nods and shrugs to each other, as if to indicate this was par for the course. It was the next communication from them that concerned us most, namely that we couldn't stay here. Well of course time had gone on and it would now be impossible to get anywhere else. Eventually we comprehended that they were telling us that there was a place quite near, just a little further on in an inlet, where we could stay. Whether it was because I did not want to give up the safety of the spot we had found for something uncertain that I pretended not to understand, or perhaps they were nice people, but they then offered to take me in their boat to show me the place and bring me back – or at least I hoped that was what they meant. What Anto must have been thinking when he watched me being taken off in their boat, leaving him alone in this desolate place, I do not know, but it may have been, what if we had misunderstood and they were taking me away to jail for tying up in the wrong place or entering their country without official permission?

It being a poor country, their patrol boat was not much more than a little lifeboat with a hood on and not capable of any great speed – none of your fast speedboats our officials would have had. Well, after passing two further inlets we turned in at the third, and sure enough there were three or four floating clubhouses with landing stages and a selection of boats tied up to them. He took me to the furthest one and indicated that this is where he wished us to come. It was clear that there was sufficient space and the depth was OK, so I was gradually coming to realise that they had done us a great favour, and what is more these clubhouses appeared to have chairs and tables and might serve food. Our plans for cooking an evening meal had had to be put on hold. They took me back to our boat, from where Anto had been watching with great concern for the sight of the returning police boat. The relief on his face on seeing my return was clear to see, as was the delight when I told him the good news. We thanked our uninvited guests with a gift of a bottle of wine and proceeded to relocate to this newfound safe and secure mooring.

The police might have known the owners of the clubhouse, and they might have rewarded them, because I don't know why they took us to the further one, but I am glad they did since the owners proved to be a most interesting and hospitable couple. He introduced himself as 'the Dodo' and his wife as 'the Witch'. The open-sided floating restaurant was done out in broomsticks and other witchcraft emblems, and netting hung like a spider's web. They could not speak English but their welcome was most sincere and they provided a superb meal at very little cost. During the evening we were introduced to a couple that were their friends and had a small boat. He was a professor at the university and could speak English. After much discussion we realised that with their help we would be able to effect our plans to visit Bratislava, so we arranged to stay two nights.

This gave us the next day to spend in the city. It was Easter Sunday, a clear and sunny day. The Dodo arranged a taxi for us to take us into Bratislava and to collect us to bring us back, and advanced us Slovakian currency on the basis that whatever we used would go on our bill, which we could pay in deutschmarks. We spent another enjoyable evening with Dodo, his wife and the professor and his wife and discussed the rest of our voyage to Budapest.

Our next convenient stopping place, the only one, was Esztergom, 148 kilometres further on in Hungary, and would involve passing through customs at Komarno – the Slovakian customs to go out and the Hungarian customs to enter. In addition, before that there was the biggest lock on the Danube to clear. With all this in mind we therefore set off the next day at 06.30 and both Dodo and his wife got up early to wave us off and wish us well, dressed in their traditional costumes. After much waving and taking photographs we were off on a long day, having enjoyed their wonderful hospitality. Dodo knew the lock keeper at the big lock at Gabeikovo and had promised to telephone him and ask him to look out for us and hopefully give us priority since the waiting time could often be very lengthy.

The Danube spreads out very wide in this part; it was misty but we had no difficulty in following the well-buoyed channel through what seemed like a sea, with the buoys mounted on little man-made islands. It then entered into a wide canal to avoid a great deal of winding river. The canal between Hungary and Slovakia had been built quite recently to avoid the much-meandering river.

We arrived at the lock at 09.15 and although we had to wait a short time we were through by 10.15. We had had to wait to go through with a tug pushing three barges, so despite the size of the lock there was not a lot of room at the back of the lock for us to fit, but the lock keeper called us in and maybe this was because of Dodo's telephone call. We were so close to the rear gates that we only had the use of one floating bollard and had to use the ladder rungs in the wall at the bow end to fasten to as we dropped down – back to leapfrogging, but much easier going down. For some reason all this was done under the watchful eyes of hundreds of spectators who lined the rails of the bridge on top of the lock gates; they must have been passengers from a cruise boat or a coach tour, we assumed. From the lock we continued following the three-barge pusher until we arrived at Komarno at 13.00. Here we knew we had to stop.

First of all the Slovakian customs pontoon on the left side of the river; again this meant going past and turning to come upriver, all of which was made more difficult by the fact that there was a bridge nearby joining Komarno on the Slovakian side with Komarom on the Hungarian side. The bridge supports had to be avoided and there was the risk of the current taking you against them. We positioned our biggest and best fenders, and despite the buffeting of the wash, reminding me of my younger days travelling on the Mersey ferry and their landing at the Liverpool landing stage, we managed to come alongside and make secure without damage at the first attempt.

Collecting the briefcase with all the documentation I set off to do the business at the customs office, but locating it was more difficult than one might expect. First I walked along the bank under the bridge in the direction of what seemed an official-looking building. Yes it did bear the country's official crest but again nobody was about. I located two soldiers, who motioned me in the direction up on the road bridge. When I got up there, there was a long line of traffic waiting to go through a custom point to cross the bridge into Hungary. I spoke to the man in the booth and mentioned I was from the river, whereupon he pointed me to go into the office. At the counter I again explained with gestures that I was on a boat. Having looked at all our papers, in which they took very little interest, they indicated it was OK to proceed. I returned to the boat along the lengthy pathway and felt relieved that we had cleared one hurdle. Anto could not understand why I did not walk across the bridge to the Hungarian side and deal with their customs there. I was of the view that this would not be acceptable and we had to move the boat across the river to their customs pontoon, tie up, locate the office and do all the business again with them. This involved of course going upriver and then turning downriver and then upriver again to moor.

Taking a route in the form of a figure of eight at the same time as being careful not to drift down into the bridge supports, it was also wise for us to move over to the opposite side of the boat our biggest and best fenders. The Hungarian pontoon was more difficult since it had collected a large quantity of driftwood entangled in its securing ropes. One wondered why a country that was trying to encourage tourist visitors did not make life easier for them. At the next pontoon was moored a fast speedboat clearly marked 'river police' which was a sufficient deterrent to discourage any idea of not bothering to stop, since clearly they were in a position to race after you. Our first attempt was at the wrong angle, too acute, but the driftwood was a big problem. On the second attempt we made it, although the bollards were very badly located for our securing to.

When we had tied up, off I went again with all the papers; fortunately Dodo and the professor had told us the direction to go since there was no indication. A man in uniform was leaning out of the window of a building watching our three-barge pusher trying to tie up. I found the entrance to the building round the other side. An untidily dressed man in uniform came forward and asked for passports, which he stamped without delay. I was about to turn round and leave but he stopped me and explained that I must see the two men who were sitting in another room watching TV. They sat me down in a spare chair and produced a form for me to complete, on which I had to enter details of the captain and the crew etc. The form was in Hungarian, but with their help and arm gestures, the various questions were answered and I was free to go, feeling that it had been quite easy, but they then made it clear that I needed to go to another building, namely the customs next door.

Well, "what were you?" I thought. Down the road I went in accordance with their directions to where they said a green car would be, and sure enough they were right. I entered this large building. There was nobody to be seen. I wandered around, knocking on every door, until at last I found what appeared to be the solitary occupant of this large building – the man I had seen leaning out of the window. Although I entered the room, he sent me out again and along the corridor to be dealt with through a little sliding window, to do the matter properly. He examined the ship's papers and asked questions in Hungarian. It was clear he could not understand a word of the documents, and when he pointed to the name and address of the builders – appearing to enquire whether this was me – I said yes since it seemed to be the simplest course of action. Shortly after this, once I had explained that we were going to Esztergom and Budapest, he indicated it was OK to go. I gratefully returned to the ship, holding aloft the briefcase by the handle like the Chancellor of the Exchequer outside No 11 on the day of his budget, as a sign to Anto everything was in order.

As soon as I was back aboard the ship we set off, being careful to change over the courtesy flag from Slovakia to Hungary. We had no locks to concern ourselves about and just one stop at Esztergom before we would reach Budapest, which was to be our resting place for a time, at least until the problems created by the Bosnian war had been overcome. Although peace had been restored, bridges at Novi Sad near Belgrade had been bombed, making it impossible for navigation through that part of the Danube. We continued our way under a clear and sunny sky to Esztergom, famous for its inspiring domed cathedral sited on a cliff above the town, looking as impressive as St Paul's in London. The bridge across the Danube here had been partly dismantled, although it looked bombed, with the forming of the country following the First World War. It had now been agreed to reconnect the two sides, and they were still in the process of doing this. As a result of the work there was a complicated and confusing buoyage system.

Dodo had told us that there was a convenient little boat harbour up an inlet, which would suit us. It was backing upriver and required a wide sweep to come back into it. At the entrance, most inconveniently sited, was a houseboat, which took up half the width of the inlet, which was already very narrow, and I was most concerned as to the depth. There was then a low bridge, which necessitated us quickly lowering the mast and the cockpit cover. I was loath to go up further and find no space for us to moor and no room to turn round, so we hurriedly tied up unofficially to the houseboat. I leapt ashore to see who I could find. I was lucky that the man in charge of this haven happened to be there and doing some repair work on his boat. He assured me it was deep enough and yes it would be possible to turn round and yes there was room, although the berth was on a very rickety pontoon.

I dashed back to the boat, hoping nobody had complained yet that we had taken a liberty to tie up. Anto would have kept out of sight and claimed not to understand. We were untied and away before anybody came. With the help of the owner we were soon secure and connected up to electricity and felt relaxed, leaving until tomorrow the concern about turning round and getting out of this narrow inlet, negotiating the low bridge and getting into the river again. After a very long and busy day of nearly twelve hours we were more than happy to be there and celebrated with a meal out in a nearby restaurant. The following day we decided to have a day off and visit the cathedral. It was a lovely sunny day.

It was a misty day with poor visibility when we set off for Budapest at 09.30, completing the necessary manoeuvre of turning round in our own length at the same time as being careful not to be taken with the current and smash smaller boats tied up along the same pontoon. Having cleared the low bridge and raised the mast and the cockpit, it was full steam ahead for Budapest. Having been overtaken by the *Mozart*, one of the best cruise ships on the river Danube and operated by the top class Peter Deilman Cruises, we fell in behind and thought there was no better company to have for our arrival in Budapest.

The Viking Marina is located at 1652 and required us to take a wide turn back into the inlet and slack water. Our arrival time at 13.45 gave plenty of time to secure and do the introductions. This was to be our resting place for we knew not how long; until the Danube was made navigable again for us to reach the Black Sea, our voyage was suspended. I was not concerned. Budapest had still not yet become a destination for no-frills airlines and it still had an atmosphere unspoiled by too many tourists. To have the opportunity to pay regular visits, with free accommodation available and the opportunity to enjoy inexpensive good quality restaurants and the opera, was an attractive proposition.

There was only one snag: visiting ships from other countries were only allowed to stay in Hungary for a maximum period of six months. Under no circumstances would it be possible for the bombed bridges that were blocking the river further on to be repaired for at least twelve to eighteen months. Surely there must be some way of obtaining some extension of the time allowed to stay, particularly given the circumstances.

Having got this far I was not going to have the boat impounded, and it was most ill-advised to be in breach of the rules. The authorities knew exactly when we had entered the country. Three different sets of forms had been completed for three different government authorities. I made enquiries as to whom I might be able to consult to resolve this problem. After many visits to shipping companies in magnificent buildings of the 1930s, which made me recall my early working life in Liverpool, I was recommended to see a new company claiming to be able to fix all commercial problems, a 'Mr Fixit'. Their offices were impressive and it was apparent that they were in great demand to cope with the awakening that was then taking place in Hungary.

The chief executive saw me; she was a 'withit lady'. She was most helpful but came to the conclusion that after much effort and consideration about re-registering the boat in Hungry and numerous other possibilities, there was no alternative but to accept the position. Namely to go back to Slovakia and stop in Komarno for one night and then return to Budapest for six months and continue to do this every six months. But this was not her main concern. When we were eventually to continue our voyage, we would have to go through Romania and she would not even consider driving her car through that country since she said they were likely to steal the wheels. So heaven help you in a boat. Our six-monthly trips back and forth to Slovakia would be nothing to what we would have to meet in the second half of our voyage.

Our return visits into Slovakia to satisfy the six-month stay restriction produced some interesting experiences. Not knowing where we might be able to find suitable moorings, I decided that a day trip by train from Budapest to Komarom would be worthwhile. From the train timetable I worked out that it would be possible to take the train from Budapest shortly after 08.00 in the morning, which would get me to Komarom at about 09.30. I could then walk across the bridge to Komarno on the opposite bank, which was in Slovakia. Hopefully I would have no problems at the passport control of both countries. There was a train back shortly after 16.00 so it would give me nearly seven hours to reconnoitre for a suitable berth for the boat just inside Slovakia. The charts showed an industrial inlet a little up river from Komarno, which can usually provide a suitable place. So on the chosen day I took the train as planned, experienced no trouble with the frontier controls on the bridge, and set off to walk to the inlet.

The entrance to it from the river was barred by a road bridge, which looked as if it had not been opened for years. The inlet had been the site of a ship builder, which had apparently gone out of business many years ago, so this proved to be a no-go idea. I could see on the river map that there was a small yacht club further up the main river just before a railway bridge and I set off to walk the distance of about three kilometres. It had become a hot day but I quite soon arrived at what at first sight looked very promising.

There were two pontoons, one looking very sturdy and the other comprising a converted barge secured to the bank by a not very stable walkway. Around this structure were a collection of motley boats. It soon became obvious to me that the first pontoon was for the army and access to it was clearly prohibited; the other was the yacht club's property.

A clubhouse on top of the river bank was the obvious port

of call and despite the fact that nobody there was able to speak English and I did not know a word of Slovakian, the club steward and his wife welcomed me very warmly. It was not every day that an odd-looking Englishman dropped in. The club secretary had happened to call in for lunch, and over a beer I managed to explain our need for an overnight mooring for a night sometime in the future. We went to their pontoon, which was in fact two barges decked and fastened together, with a nasty bit very inconveniently protruding in the middle as part of the joining structure, which later proved an inconvenient obstacle. The total combined length of the two together was about 14 metres (the length of our boat) and they would be happy to make space for us by moving any of their members' boats round the back.

They seemed very proud that they might have a British boat of such size visiting their club but I was concerned that the 16-ton weight with the force of the river might take the whole structure away from the bank. It was not possible to use the army's pontoon under any circumstances, I was told in response to my enquiry.

All I had to do was contact them and give plenty of warning; they would be delighted to provide the much-needed overnight stopping just inside Slovakia. Telephone and fax numbers were duly noted and I left to walk back, pass through passport control out of Slovakia in Komarno, walk over the bridge, go through passport control into Komarom in Hungary and then to the train station to return to Budapest.

I arrived at the station in plenty of time, feeling mission accomplished. The train track, for a great deal of the time, ran along the side of the river and one was able to see a stretch that I was subsequently to be covering six times.

When the time came for us to make our first voyage back up

river, we knew that it would take two days to get to Komarom and one day to get back. Three days in total with two night stopovers: one on the way up in the little creek at Esztergom with the inconveniently situated houseboat at the mouth, then the low bridge and the wonky pontoons; the second night at our clubhouse in Komarno after going through the two lots of customs formalities, repeating this the next day before taking the leisurely cruise back past Santandor to our semi-permanent berth in Budapest.

Going back up river instead of carrying on the way we wanted to go seemed stupid but was necessary. The checking in and out of Slovakia and out and into Hungary and the changing of the courtesy flag midstream became routine, although coming alongside any berth on the Danube can never be taken as routine. We still have one nasty little dint to the rim of the hull as a record of when an impatient and sarcastic remark from a crew member disturbed normal judgement and we came in too fast. On our first visit to Komarno yacht club the pre-notification arrangement worked and they prepared the pontoon for our arrival. Once secure, pleasantries were exchanged and the club secretary and a couple of other members appreciated coming aboard and seeing the ship.

Also whilst they were appreciating our hospitality and whisky we established in conversation that the club provided evening meals and we were welcome to partake. Not wanting to miss the opportunity of sampling their food and also wanting to support the club, we accepted, although with a little trepidation as to what the menu might offer.

It was suggested that we might like to try the 'House Special', a delicacy of Slovakia for which a name was given but meant nothing to us. Anto, more adventurous with regard to food being the chef, accepted without hesitation; I was more inquisitive and after much sign language, we established the primary item for this dish was bull's penis. Even Anto changed his mind!

On a subsequent visit we opted to stay for two nights to give us an opportunity to learn about Komarno in case there might be something we were missing. The club secretary arranged for us to have an English-speaking guide to take us round. When Czechoslovakia was divided, there was no doubt that Slovakia ended up with the much poorer half. The Romans had created a fortress as part of their chain of 'Limes' along the right bank of the Danube, which included Komarom. Komarno was on the side of the Danube occupied by the Barbarians and would appear to have always been the poor relation. The two towns were strategically positioned, but Komarno has been shunted in and out of Czechoslovakia over the years. Following the disintegration of the Austro-Hungarian Empire, it became part of Czechoslovakia, whereas Komarom remained in Hungary. In 1939 Komarno was annexed back into Hungary but after the Second World War returned to Czechoslovakia.

Our stopover in Esztergom was always fraught with the difficulties of turning round in the small side river. In the autumn when the water was low, the problem was depth and not to get stuck on the bottom. In the spring when the water was high and running fast, we had to overcome being swept downriver when broadside and smashing into other boats.

There was a selection of interesting restaurants to choose from and an interesting town centre, but after the fourth time of having to visit the town, we had seen enough of it.

The River Danube.

The Iron Gorge – River Danube.

Miltenburg – River Main.

Ready to leave – the boat builders in Sneek.

The crew resting at Rousse Yacht Club.

In port. Vienna.

The bombed bridge at Novi Sad.

The Istanbul end of the Bosphorus.

On our numerous visits to Budapest over the two years the boat was moored there, we had plenty of opportunities to enjoy this interesting city. This was before the spate of cheap flights now available, and our route had to involve flying from London and then going by taxi to the boat.

Once we decided to take a five-day visit to Lake Balaton and took a train to Heviz and joined the large number of the more elderly members of the population who enjoy the health-giving properties provided by the waters of the lake, which is fed by an underwater spring and the temperature of the water never falls below 30 degrees centigrade.

The hotel was more like a hospital, with treatment rooms and water baths providing cures for various ailments. The food offered was very health conscious and the protein content of each course was evaluated and shown on the menu. The lake itself gave off a strong sulphurous smell, and round the side were enclosures providing seating and eating areas, but more importantly, wooden decking and jetties, from which you could enter the water. Most people sat in rubber rings and bobbed about like a sea of corks. A small rowing boat with a red cross on the side hovered round in the centre of the lake in which a lifeguard scanned the scene, ready to pick out anybody who might appear to be in difficulty. It reminded me of the fairground stall where you pick out floating corks with a small fishing rod in the hope of selecting a lucky number. The buoyancy of the water was such that it appeared virtually impossible to sink; there was no shallow part; it was deep even at the side so if you were a non-swimmer, you had to have confidence in the water's properties. The fir trees and vegetation surrounding the lake and the style of the buildings created an alpine-type setting and was perfect walking country.

The fact that Hungary had been under Communist rule up to a few years before was still very apparent, particularly in the suburbs with drab, multi-storey, poorly built tenement blocks. However, it was also the era of classic twenties architecture which was very apparent in the baroque buildings and wide, tree-lined boulevards, but all very much in need of repair. It was a poor man's Paris where we could enjoy fine meals and the opera at a fraction of the cost back home. We could get into the centre of Budapest from the boat by public transport in half an hour: a short walk to the electric train station nearby (the trains ran every 15 minutes with one change, using a train which went under the river, two more stops) and you were bang in the centre. Whereas we got to know a number of good restaurants, particularly the famous Gundals, we were fortunate that within walking distance of the boat was a square that had been the first stop on the stage-coach route from Budapest to Vienna where a number of coaching inns had sprung up. A few still operated and had retained their character; one had a collection of antiques that made it more of a museum. Our favourite was the Postakocsi, which had a stage-coach theme. Pictures, lamps, even the tables, were positioned like horseboxes to recall the bygone age. The food was delicious and often accompanied by gypsy music. They made a duck dish in a Hungarian red wine, which was a memorable meal.

Apart from food, the other recreation which provided us with endless enjoyment was the spa baths. In the winter, the best were the famous Gellert Baths where the architecture provided a magnificent setting. There was a communal pool for men and women, with an arched roof, pictures of which are commonplace in advertising Budapest. Separate sections were then available for men and women where clothing was reduced to a minimal piece of modesty cloth, which did little to fulfil its function. Here there were two further pools, one constantly 33 degrees centigrade and the other just a couple of degrees cooler. In addition, a cold plunge and a steam room, in which you literally cooked, with a row of massage tables more akin to mortuary slabs, on which you were pummelled and then literally hosed down; after this you felt like a new pin. In the summer months we would visit the out-door baths which were situated on Margaret Island in the centre of the river, rather than the well-photographed one which was on the other side of town. Here, similar facilities existed, but out of doors, and the steam rose from the water into the hot air above a cloudless blue sky.

Budapest enjoys very hot summer weather but the winters are extremely cold, with ice and snow on the ground for at least two months. The contrasts are extreme, but needless to say, our time in Budapest was put to good use.

PART 2

CHAPTER 8

RIVER DANUBE

– BUDAPEST TO MOHÁCS AND INTO SERBIA

It was a spring day when we flew back to Budapest for the last time to continue our epic voyage along the river Danube to the Black Sea and eventually to Istanbul.

Our voyage from Sneek in the north of Holland via the River Ems, the Rhine, the Marne and the Main-Danube canal to the River Danube had been suspended in Budapest in 2000. It was now two years later. The reason for the extended stopover had now been removed and I was confident it was safe to go on.

Budapest had been a superb location to have a *pied-à-terre*, with very hot summers but severe winters when temperatures fall to below zero for up to four months. During this time it had been necessary to have the boat taken out of the water and cocooned, at considerable expense, to protect it from the freezing conditions. I was relieved that this would now be avoided in the future. For most of the year, however, Budapest had provided us with some great times, with the opportunity to visit the fine baroque Opera House and enjoy superb performances at a fraction of the price in London, as well as to enjoy the relaxation of the spa waters, which were two of many amenities we had come to enjoy. Our favourite location for dining was at the fine restaurant Gundals, and this had to be a must on the last night before we set off. A fixed menu of eight courses, with a different wine served with each course and included in the price. As with most Hungarian restaurants, live music was provided, but at Gundals the music, provided by a quartet of superb quality, was like wine to the ear. The Viking Marina, at just four stops north on the green electric train line, had been the location of the Budapest ship building yard many years before. It had now been converted into a fast-growing marina, as the economy of Hungary improved and more people could afford boats.

Back onboard again was exciting and this time we had to make sure everything was in working order. The extreme winter weather had had its effects, and four out of the six batteries were considered not to be up to scratch and replacements were necessary. Apart from that everything seemed fine. We had managed to tighten up our windscreen wipers, which we remembered had been slipping towards the end of the last trip, since when no use had been required of them. Now they would be important. We had brought back with us from England a large quantity of easily packed food, soup powders and the like, but stocking up with food was our prime consideration. So off we went with all manner of empty bags – kit bags, holdalls and the like – to the supermarket some five kilometres away. Supermarkets all the world over have a similarity; many things can be identified by sight but without a knowledge of Hungarian it took us some time to work out what was what. Eventually, laden down with twelve bags full to capacity, the three of us struggled back to the boat with our stores. Bottles of water, plenty of drink, fruit, vegetables and meat can be very heavy.

Our next task was to fill up the boat with fuel and water, and to do this the boat had to be moved to where the fuel pumps were located. Everything takes so long with boats for some reason. It is not like pulling into a filling station in a car. What should have taken an hour or so took three hours. Initially there was the need to have four boats moved, which were tied up in the way. This provided sufficient room for us to tie alongside the part of the quay near enough for the fuel and water hoses to reach us.

When the boat had been built I had foreseen the potential problem of refuelling during part of our planned voyage. I had struck on the idea of having the void space in the bathing platform made into a spare fuel tank which could take an extra 500 gallons in addition to the 2,000 gallons in our main tanks. This later proved to be invaluable.

The last time I had moved the boat from the quay to refill the fresh water tanks had been the previous autumn, when the water in the river had fallen to such a low level that I had struggled to steer the boat and many times got stuck on the bottom. There was no such difficulty this time, as the melting snow and the spring rains had lifted the river level.

We could take the boat out from the side river where the marina was situated into the main river and give it a good run. In addition to myself and my companion Anto, who together with me had brought the boat from Holland, we had invited a third person, Neil, to join us on this second section, hopefully to ease the strain and help with the workload.

Once we were eventually in the right position, whilst Anto dealt with the filling of thc water, Neil and I set about the refuelling with the help of the marina staff and met our first major problem. The extreme temperature variations had somehow had an effect on the fuel caps. They were impossible to unscrew and their position was such that it was not possible to get a wrench onto them. Despite a variety of tools being used to get them to shift, it was impossible. Eventually somehow we succeeded and refuelling could commence. With full tanks and £250 lighter we returned to our berth knowing that provided we got the replacement batteries delivered we would be able to set off the following day.

The batteries did arrive at 17.00, so the next morning, Saturday 1 June, bright and early in blazing sunshine, we set off from what had been our home base for two years. This period had been broken up into six-monthly sessions by short trips up the Danube into Slovakia to satisfy the requirements that we could only stay a maximum of six months in Hungary. These visits had been minor events in themselves and required an overnight stop on the way upstream at Esztergom, since it took us two days to get out of Hungary at Komarom in order to stay in Slovakia at least one night at the sister town of Komarno on the opposite bank, which is in Slovakia.

There was some feeling of nostalgia as we sailed off. The owner of the marina and his son were there to wave us off and wish us well, and many of the staff, whom we had got to know well, joined in with their well-wishing. Reflecting on the fact that during our eighteen-month stay, with berthing fees, wintering, repairs, new batteries, fuel etc, we must have spent the equivalent of about £5,000 with them, they must have felt some disappointment at the loss of our valuable custom.

Sailing past the magnificent riverside buildings in Budapest, such as the Houses of Parliament, and under the majestic bridges of this lovely city which we had come to consider our second home, Anto and I both expressed a sense of sadness as we waved it goodbye.

As previously experienced, the problem with the river Danube is finding suitable stopping places for over-nighting. Much studying of the chart books and working out distances to plan the itinerary is called for, with a fallback position required if intended stopping places do not materialise as suitable. A yacht club was shown at Dunaföldvár, a comfortable 90 kilometres from Budapest, which would make an ideal distance for the first day. I had faxed the owner asking whether it might be possible for us to stay, and he had kindly telephoned me back to say it would be fine by him. So it was comforting to think we would be expected.

During nearly five hours of easy going, we passed few ships coming the other way, one of which was blue-flagging (this requires that we have to pass on the opposite side to normal, which is port to port, and enables big ships to maximise the width of the river at difficult bends). As we approached the position where the yacht club was located we could see flags waving on poles set back from the river, but despite scouring the bank through binoculars we could not see the entrance to any inlet.

Suddenly we spotted a small boat coming out towards us with two men waving their arms, indicating the route we were to follow into their small haven, which we could not have seen. They had reserved a special pontoon just inside the entrance, manned by what seemed to be the entire committee. The owner's name proved to be Charlie, and he turned out to be an Angel. Once secured, we were ready to greet our hosts, and much handshaking and expressing our thanks for their help in piloting us followed. We found that Charlie was the only member who could speak English; having been a lorry driver, which had involved him in journeys all over Europe, he had equipped himself well for these trips. He took great delight in telling us many times of the difficulties he had experienced when ordering beer until he realised the correct pronunciation of 'ale'; he had been asking for 'alley'.

The hospitality extended to us on this our first night's stop was not to be equalled. An exploratory walk into the nearby town revealed little of interest. On returning to the yacht club we found Charlie had arranged with the local TV station for us to be interviewed on camera. The three of us sat with Charlie and the boat behind, whilst the interviewer and interpreter conducted a question-and-answer session in front of the TV cameras. We were told the interview would go out on the local TV programme the next night, but we never did ascertain whether this in fact happened, but we still felt famous.

That evening, the clubhouse provided an ideal venue for our evening meal, a Hungarian meal of chicken goulash whilst Charlie serenaded us on his mouth organ. We appreciated the significance of the name International since there were ten different nationalities represented in the clubhouse that evening.

We had planned to leave the next day at 09.00, and before saying goodnight, Charlie, having consumed much ale, had offered to come to the yacht club at 08.30. He was concerned about the shallow water round the entrance to the inlet and promised to pilot us out through the narrow channel. As a result we had not paid a great deal of attention as to the location of this channel. At 9.30 Charlie had still not shown up and time was going on. We collectively managed to recall that he had mentioned something about right angles from the bank, so having thanked his wife and left her with a bottle of wine for Charlie we decided to go it alone. Having made sure the river was clear of other boats, we shot out in reverse into midstream before turning downstream to continue on our way to our next planned stopping place at Baja, again some 90 kilometres distant.

By comparison to the Rhine, the Danube would be considered a C road if the Rhine were a motorway. We passed only two commercial boats going upstream on our trip to Baja. From my research I had ascertained that there was a hotel-cum-camping site with a mooring down a small canal off the main river. We preferred where possible to moor off the main river, since it is more restful and you are less likely to be disturbed by the wash of the few passing barges. As we arrived at Baja we noticed a small wall which would suit us for mooring should our small canal not prove deep enough. We turned to come upstream into the canal and were delighted to find it had a depth of four metres, so there was no problem. We edged along in accordance with the directions they had provided when acknowledging my faxed booking. Taking a right and left we came upon a deserted landing stage and assumed this must be it. It was just the right length and provided sufficient depth, so our luck was holding and our preparations were paying off.

I walked through the grounds to the hotel reception which welcomed me with expectation and requested the fee of 200 Florins, the equivalent of £5, plus an extra 75p for electricity. A bargain and very helpful because we would not need to use valuable fuel stock on the generator. It transpired that the electricity supply was nearly 200 metres from the boat, so our extension lead came in handy.

By planning to get to our stopping places by 16.00 if possible, we had time for a walk before dinner to see what the local town might provide in the way of shops, bars and restaurants etc. Well in Baja there was little to write home about in that respect but we did watch a large religious festival being enacted in the town square. With a hotel being at hand we again took the lazy option of not cooking, and preserved our food stock. It was cheap but not very good.

The following morning we were relieved to find that the water level in the river had not dropped in the night, which would have caused us problems in returning to the river, since we had only about nine inches of water below the keel. We were soon steaming along at a steady 10 knots, bound for Mohács, the border town between Hungary and Serbia.

As we approached Mohács we could see a small landing stage with a police boat moored, but no sign of a stage for the Hungarian customs. A large barge permanently secured had access to the bank, so we chose to moor up to that. A police boat had moved out into the river and was keeping a close watch on our efforts; they then came alongside and explained to us the need to report to the Hungarian customs here, and further on to the Serbian authorities. We were fully aware of this, but pleased to have this confirmation that we were in the right place, and thanked them. The owner of the barge then appeared on the other side of our boat and began gesturing that we could not moor against his barge, but his objections were soon dispelled when I showed him some money and assured him we would see him right.

Once we were fully secured, our by then welcoming host set off on his moped, leading Neil and me to the customs office. This proved to be set well back and not easily visible from the river. He took us first to the police, where two officers completed the appropriate form and examined our documents. Seeing my place of birth on my passport as Liverpool, he referred, as often happens, to football and reeled off a collection of English footballers' names. This helped to break the ice and relax the officialdom. Our helpful host then took us upstairs to another more organised office where the official stamped our passports, filled out a couple more forms and bade us on our way.

We returned to the boat pleased that we had passed through the first of our border controls. As we approached, our helpful host had made himself very conspicuous, polishing his bike lest we overlooked our promise. A bottle of whisky and our thanks left him happy as we left to do battle at the next frontier post into Serbia.

A further 12 kilometres on was its location and again we had difficulty in recognising the place. There were no signs, but a large ship tied up at a pontoon gave us the tip that this must be the place. The ship fortunately moved away as we arrived, leaving us room to come alongside helped by two men who were employed to help tie up, for which a fee of US$5 was due. Neil and I left Anto to look after the boat in the company of the two stagehands, engaged in fishing, to locate the Serbian authorities this time. We were sent in the direction of a large office block over a much-worn and dilapidated bridge linking the pontoon to the bank. We were confronted by many doors along the corridor when we arrived in the building, none of which gave any indication as to the room we needed, with the exception of one which said 'police', so we tried that one. We appeared to be interrupting their television viewing and after a cursory examination of our passports they directed us to an unnamed door where again we found ourselves interrupting the watching of a football match on the TV. I explained we had a boat and wanted to see the Port Captain, whereupon a delightful man sat us down and commenced the laborious task of completing three separate forms in quadruplicate, running to a total of 24 sheets of paper, each time carefully securing the carbon paper between the copies and retaining the paper together with paper clips in each corner. Fortunately he spoke English. Eventually, when completed, a payment of 30 florins was required, but he was not authorised to accept payment of this fee. It had to be made at an officially designated border crossing, but being the nice guy he was he took me in his clapped out old Skoda car at breakneck speed to a roadside customs point for the transaction to be effected and evidenced with a similar quadruplicate form filling. Back I then went to his office, where I had left Neil. Anto was on the boat, so we were all spread about in an effort to effect our entry into the first of the countries we had to pass through.

Once back at his office it was necessary for him to have the forms authorised by his superior. He then provided us with one copy of all the forms to surrender on our leaving Serbia. He had granted us 30 days to complete our journey through Serbia. But it was not over yet. He then took us back to the police who this time did examine our passports more thoroughly and stamped them. Anticipating the possible problem over obtaining visas at the frontier, I had made the point of visiting the Yugoslavian Embassy in London before we left, and had acquired the necessary visas for the three of us, which as it turned out may not have been necessary but will have certainly saved another hour of extensive form filling.

We returned to the boat, where we had left Anto two hours before, thinking we could set off, but the two men who were keeping Anto company said no. We still had to wait for the customs to come and clear us. How long would that be? we asked. "Don't know – any time," was their response, "would you like some fish?" Eventually, after waiting a further hour, all of the people we had already seen appeared, along with the customs official, and asked to come aboard and look around. This required the production of all the papers and passports again.

The customs official's main preoccupation was to ascertain how much money we were bringing into the country. Having completed the necessary form we were given a copy to add to the pile we had already acquired. After handshakes all round they left us and we set off promptly in case they changed their minds or had forgotten to complete yet another form.

CHAPTER 9

RIVER DANUBE THROUGH SERBIA

It would take us a further two or three hours from the Serbian frontier to reach Apatin, which I had selected as the next suitable overnight stopping place. The chart indicated a haven down a side inlet on the left bank, which would hopefully provide a suitable mooring. A crane, a shipyard and a ski club were all shown as being there so we were hopeful. As we approached, a tug was pushing a barge into the inlet, which was comforting since it indicated that there was sufficient depth.

How far into the inlet the deep water would exist, however, was uncertain, so when the captain of the tug confirmed as OK our request to tie up alongside the barge we quickly made fast to it. Once secure I walked down the side of the barge to express my thanks to the captain of the tug, whereupon he made it clear that he was leaving, having delivered the barge, and it was up to us if we chose to stay. Other members of the crew, however, made it very clear that they thought we would be ill-advised to stay there. So we untied and gingerly explored further into the inlet. Passing a motley collection of small boats with no suitable landing stages we came to the shipyard, which gave the impression of being derelict. There was a quay with a rusting old ship tied up to it which we could go alongside, and it would be a reasonable place to spend the night with a view to an early start next day.

Past experience has shown that in these circumstances if anything is going to happen it will be whilst we are eating, so we decided it would be advisable to have our dinner early. Sure enough, before we had finished we spotted that a man in overalls had arrived and was looking us over. Our initial plan was to ignore him at least until we had finished eating, by which time another man had joined him.

Again experience has shown that problems don't go away and are best dealt with sooner rather than later when it might have gone dark, so outside we went to confront them. Despite our pleas, one was adamant that we could not stay whereas the other one, under the inducement of whisky and the offer of cash, was more prepared to close his eyes to us. After much persuasion they agreed to go and telephone their boss to see what he might say.

After about twenty minutes they returned to say he had agreed it would be OK just for one night. We were relieved and thanked them with a glass of whisky each, but hardly had they drained their glasses when to their dismay and ours a policeman came into view coming down the quay.

Fortunately we could say that we had the permission of the owner to stay there, but that of course was not sufficient. "Let me see your papers," he demanded.

A thorough examination of our papers and the sheaf of forms provided when we arrived in the country was made, and then I was asked to accompany him to the police station in another dilapidated Skoda. The journey was through the shipyard, which although giving the appearance of dereliction was in operation and had a formidable gatehouse. The policeman impatiently sounded his horn as we approached and the gatekeeper ran out to open the gate in response to his summons.

At the police station it was obvious to us from a chart on the wall that both our policeman and his colleague on duty were at the bottom of a list of 20 in rank. They proceeded to examine the documents we had been provided with on entry into Serbia, with which they appeared to be unfamiliar and carefully read every word on the 12 sheets, examined our passports and visas and frequently consulted higher authority by telephone.

Eventually they appeared sufficiently satisfied and indicated they would take us back to the boat. However they needed to take photocopies of all of the 12 pages of the documents. Their first efforts resulted in the copy being chewed up by the machine, requiring them to dismantle the machine and reassemble it before they were successful in obtaining their required copies. They took the two of us back to the boat through the heavily guarded factory gatehouse. We reflected on the fact that we had spent something in the region of four hours in total in offices of the authorities in one day, and at this rate it was going to take a long time to complete our voyage.

We had been asked to sound the boat horn when we were leaving the next morning, and it was made clear that we were required to report to the authorities each night at our stopping places in Serbia.

The access bridge to the old rusting ship acting as a pontoon was so old and rusty one felt it would collapse as one walked along it, so we were relieved to get back on board and turn in for the night.

One could be forgiven for thinking the matter of police and officialdom would stop here, but no. At about midnight I was awakened by heavy footsteps on deck, lights flashing and voices shouting "Police". I jumped up and looked through the open skylight, but with the mosquito guard in place I could not make out who was there and felt it might be impostors or troublemakers. I removed the mosquito protection so that I could see them and converse from the safety of the inside of the locked boat. They shone their torch onto their badges to confirm their authenticity and showed me through the opening a copy of the papers which we had received on our entry into Serbia, on which my signature clearly appeared. They appeared to be saying that I should have reported to the police station, to which I was responding in a language equally foreign to them that we had reported to the police station and spent two hours there, so please go away, leave us alone and let us get back to sleep.

After ten minutes of this interchange they appeared to get the message and went off. The following morning we got up early and left at 07.00, anxious to be on our way before more police arrived. We did as requested and gave three very loud blasts on the horn as we passed by the police station, but nobody appeared or seemed interested.

Waking up early was no problem since the shipyard, far from being derelict, had started in full swing at 06.00, banging and riveting. Our journey for the day was to be the longest so far: 143 kilometres (90 miles) to Novi Sad through Vukovar, which had suffered formidable bombing and destruction during the Bosnian War.

It was at Novi Sad that all of the four bridges across the Danube had been bombed, which was the reason for our delay in continuing our journey to Istanbul. Whereas they had repaired two of the bridges and partly cleared the others, a floating roadway had been constructed across the river as a temporary measure. This had in effect become permanent. Its obstruction was used as a bargaining tool in extracting the necessary funds from the countries responsible for destroying the bridges to meet the cost of repairs and reinstatement.

They had during the last year introduced the practice of opening the bridge once a week to let river traffic through. This was on Saturday night at midnight, and it was left open until noon on Sunday. Prior to that, it had been only once a month. So we knew that we could get through provided we were there at the right time.

We had researched the location, particularly since we knew we might have to wait a few days here, and we were aware that just prior to the last remaining broken bridge there was an inlet with recreational facilities and boat moorings. Although we had pictures of this from the land we had difficulty in seeing the entrance from the river. So we were just about to abort our search and go on through the bridge with a view to trying our luck at the alternative mooring – namely a rowing club pontoon further on – when we saw the entrance. We did an emergency stop and an about-turn virtually on top of the broken bridge segments over which we were gingerly advancing, and turned into the inlet. At the entrance was a floating café bar with railings around, and seats and tables for customers.

Being concerned that further in might be too shallow, we pulled alongside the front of this pontoon, taking up the whole length, made temporarily secure and proceeded to ascertain from a nice young lady who spoke perfect English whether there was any chance of being able to moor up here. She said she would telephone the owner, and we were more than delighted when she returned and confirmed that he was agreeable and that he would be along at 17.00 to see us.

We made secure, being careful not to damage any part of the terrace. When the owner arrived his expression seemed to indicate that perhaps he had not fully appreciated the size of the boat; we effectively blocked the view of the entire river for his customers. He was more than kind, and with the nice waitress acting as interpreter, confirmed we could stay as long as necessary and we could connect up our electricity supply and fill up with water. Whether the fact that we had made a point of frequenting his bar and being seen to be customers on his arrival had anything to do with it we would never know.

We went out into the town for dinner but first this time made sure to report and produce our documents to the police; they were more than pleasant and took very little time to complete the inspection. As long as they knew the exact point on the river where we had stopped they indicated we could stay as many nights as were necessary provided we stopped by and told them on our departure. They were also able to confirm the opening times on Saturday night and that there was now an extra time, namely 22.00 Wednesday until 05.00 Thursday, which was of course that very night until early the next day. We decided we were ahead of schedule and could benefit from a rest and did not look kindly on the possibility of getting up in the middle of the night. We would wait until Saturday.

Later that night, having enjoyed a superb meal at a floating restaurant near the floating roadway from where we were able to see it open, we then enjoyed a good night's sleep and a lie-in the next morning. Our next day was an opportunity to check the engines, stock up with food and rest.

We had arrived at Novi Sad earlier than expected and this

would involve staying four days, compared with the expected two. Although it was a pleasant town, we were anxious to move on. We enquired each day as to whether the bridge would be opening any earlier and were told that that night there would be an unscheduled opening at 23.00 until 04.30. We considered the possibility of getting up in the middle of the night. It would just be light by 04.00, at least enough to navigate, but a roaring gale had started and the wind was blowing at force eight. With the position of the boat and all the potential obstacles to navigate through the narrow passage between the remains of the broken bridge, it could prove very difficult. We aborted the idea of taking advantage of this opportunity and instead patiently waited until the Sunday morning.

Novi Sad had suffered severe bombing of the bridges but the town had not been affected and it still had an Eastern European atmosphere, with squares and pavement cafés with a large market and plenty of fresh produce. Our short stay at Novi Sad was coming to an end as the Saturday night opening time was now approaching. It had given us the opportunity to restock with food and to relax. The area around the boat was known as the Strand, namely the beach, and on a Saturday became alive with families and groups of youngsters playing games and sunbathing.

Many boats had taken to the water, from an elegant Chris craft to many home-made vessels. For our last evening we decided to eat onboard and take pre-dinner drinks on the terrace of our host's café pontoon so we could bid our farewells in anticipation of an early start.

When back on board we noticed that the lighting had become very dim, which we could not understand, having disconnected our shoreline electrical supply and moved over to the generator.

It being a Saturday night, the bar was busy and music was

being played at full blast so there was little opportunity to have an early night. Added to which there was the anxiety of the power supply, so sleep did not come. At midnight I was still awake. Looking out, I saw that although the music was still blaring out from the café, most of the customers had gone home. So I decided that it might be wise to reconnect the power line. The staff were surprised to see me climbing over the guardrails again, and in order for them to hear what it was I wanted they had to turn the music down. When I returned to the boat it was not turned up again, so I had unintentionally made a great achievement and sleep was possible.

At six o'clock we were all up and awake, but the shore power line had had no effect in charging up the batteries providing the lighting. The owner and the waitress had all gone home but the security man and his friend had been fishing since first light.

The starter motors are powered from different batteries from those that provide the lighting etc. and they had no difficulties in providing sufficient power to start the engines.

Clearly there was a problem with the charging system from the generator and from shore-based electricity supplies, but there was no time for us to concern ourselves about this. Now we needed to set off and negotiate the damaged bridge and get through the opened floating roadway.

Waved off by the security guard and his friend, we passed through the narrow section of the partly submerged broken bridge and round a bend in the river, and to our delight saw the gaping open section of the floating roadway. A sight we had been waiting eighteen months for. Immediately after we passed through, the police control pontoon was on the left bank. This was the place at which we had to report our departure. It was 06.00 and we slowed down to come alongside. We gave two polite toots on the horn. Nobody seemed to be about. At the third attempt a uniformed officer appeared looking very sleepy and waved us on. So with much relief we set off from Novi Sad for Belgrade, a distance of about 90 kilometres, aware that we had broken through what had been the barrier to completing our voyage.

The only event of any significance as we steamed along was the passing at 08.00 of the Peter Deilmann Cruise ship the *Mozart* going at full steam in the opposite direction in the hope of making the opened floating roadway before it closed at midday. This was the only river cruise company, which had recommenced cruising the lower parts of the Danube. We hailed them as we passed but received little response – we had to assume that they were all having breakfast or still in bed.

With so little other shipping on the river we could be forgiven for thinking that seeing us passing and flying our blue ensign might have been of interest to some of the passengers in what otherwise is a very boring section of their river cruise.

We arrived at Belgrade at 14.00 and had already decided that the best place to moor was likely to be the industrial harbour not too far from the centre of the town and quite close to the police control bureau for reporting purposes.

A large Russian-registered ship carrying motor cars was already tied up at the police control quay, so there was no room for us. Immediately after was the entrance to the industrial harbour, so in we went. It was far from full but being designed for big ships there was no place where we could tie up and be able to get off the boat onto the quay.

There was, however, a big barge moored up, and as we came close, a hand wave produced a greeting from a young lady onboard.

Anto, being Dutch, detected her accent as being that of a fellow countryman, and an exchange of conversation in their mother tongue soon established a friendly relationship. They were agreeable to our tying up alongside, which provided a means of access to land. The owners were a couple from Limburg operating their barge between Rotterdam and Belgrade. Getting from our boat onto the barge was easy but then it was necessary to climb up a vertical steel ladder set in the wall, a distance of 30 feet to the dockside. A little inconvenience but so what, we had a safe berth less than a mile from the centre of Belgrade.

The first task was to report to the police centre. On our arrival they indicated that they were already aware of our presence and exact location alongside the Dutch barge and were quite relaxed about it, so now all we had to do was find our way out of the docks into the town.

Although it was a Sunday, the market was open, and after a refreshing beer at a pavement café, we set about buying more fresh fruit and vegetables. An amusing incident occurred when buying a lettuce. We were undecided about which of two varieties to buy, and because we had handled both, the stallholder was insisting we bought both. Needless to say we bought neither. At a stall selling lettuces further on we selected one but the stallholder insisted we have an extra one free, which meant the lettuces cost 10p each, which must be a record.

Returning to the boat and carrying the shopping down the 30-foot ladder was soon completed and we rested prior to our return to the town again in the evening for a wonderful meal at a restaurant we had seen earlier. Bedecked in petunias round a little fountain, the meal and service were wonderful – hors d'oeuvres, pork medallion and salad accompanied by a local red wine, was fantastic value.

We awoke to pouring rain and a heavy cloudy sky, a complete change from the weather we had become used to. We were not distracted from our plan to leave at 07.30 and in the miserable weather untied ourselves from our friendly Dutch barge, *Progress*, and waved farewell. As we slowly made our way out of the haven into the river again the visibility was poor and we turned upstream and down again to pass the police stage. Despite our horn blowing, nobody appeared. There was a ship tied up to the stage, and we could not raise anybody to acknowledge our departure, but having made clear the previous day that our intention was to stay only one night, we felt comfortable in continuing on our way.

A conveniently situated bunker station some two kilometres from Belgrade was too good to miss. Whereas the gauge was still showing the tank to be three quarters full, gauges cannot be relied upon and it is wise to top up when the opportunity arises.

Coming alongside was not a problem, and yes, it was staffed. At first there was a negative response to our request that they provide us with fuel without a ticket which had to be obtained from a place in Belgrade, and no, they could not take credit cards. After showing money, their resolve weakened and they said they would telephone the 'Boss'. This took a considerable time and eventually things began to look more positive, and then the question arose of how much was required. We had to be influenced by the amount of Yugoslavian forints we still had left.

However, when we suggested that we would take 500 litres depending upon the price, they disappeared again into their office. It was then that we noticed that the nozzles on the pipelines were far too big to fit into the fuel inlet pipes on our boat, so perhaps we were wasting our time. After what seemed an extremely long delay to make what would appear to be a simple calculation (but then they might be debating how much to add on for themselves), they eventually reappeared and announced that we could not be served, whereupon we decided that enough was enough and left, having wasted an hour.

The journey continued with the usual routine – nothing special except that very soon we were caught up by a vessel of the Serbian navy and decided it was prudent to let them pass at the first convenient opportunity. The scenery was improving since we were approaching the Iron Gorge and the landscape on either side was more reminiscent of Austria. We passed Smederevo on the right bank, which is very famous for its sprawling castle.

Shortly before 15.00 we came to Veliko Gradište, the last place for checking out of Serbia, although we did not want to do that until the next day. We were aware that there was a quay for tying up as well as two pontoons for reporting purposes.

As we approached we could see that the quay was already well occupied with boats tied two deep, but there was a small gap just big enough for our needs. We came back upriver with a view to backing into this small place, when one of the outer boats already rafted to another beckoned that we could come alongside them, which we gladly did, and having made sufficiently fast to them, set off by crossing the two boats to deal with the formalities. We were concerned that they might check us out, which would mean we would have to leave Serbia, whereas we wanted to stay the night and leave the next day.

First the police, who despite not speaking English soon understood our wishes and gave us the OK to stay the night but report back the next morning before we left. They required another form completed exactly the same as one already filled in, but this time, in addition to being signed, it had to be stamped with the official boat stamp. In anticipation of this piece of potential bureaucracy we had had a stamp made and were not therefore caught out. In fact we were becoming disappointed since until now its use had not been called upon.

Then to the customs, who quickly waved us away since going out of the country did not seem important whereas coming in would have been. Next we went to the captain of the port, who was pleasant, and it did not take too long to complete his formalities. He retained the ship's documents, gave us a receipt for them and explained that we would get them back when we left the next day. Meanwhile we could stay and on return were asked to pay a 10-euro mooring fee.

Time for a cup of tea. Hardly had we started to drink it than the boat we were tied to announced that they were leaving, so we had to move away and this time we returned to the spot on the quay we had originally intended to go to. Having had a good meal out and an interesting evening the night before, we were quite happy to eat on board and keep watch; the weather being extremely wet made this even more attractive. Boats came and went and we were just hopeful that nobody would box us in. The weather turned nasty very suddenly. We had dinner and commented on the reduced visibility. The river here is quite wide, about a kilometre, and the other side was not in view.

The wind started to increase and very shortly was gusting at force eight, and the waves were bouncing and banging against the side of the boat and rocking us very violently. We reinforced our lines by putting out extra ropes and making sure the fenders were in the right position to ensure the boat was not damaged as we were buffeted against the quay quite violently. We felt pleased that we had ourselves securely fastened in what hopefully was a safe place, although this was the first night we were moored on the river itself rather than in an inlet or haven.

We turned in for the night feeling tired but sleep did not come easily with the violent rocking of the boat. There were two large barges tied up behind very close to our stern and a tug in front of us which had been so helpful in our mooring. They provided shelter, but suddenly we heard voices and getting out of bed we found that two bright searchlights from the old barge behind were shining at us and all her navigation lights were on. She was moving off. Hurriedly we put on our navigation lights to remind her of our presence in case by any chance she had forgotten about us. She came within a couple of inches as she edged herself out.

Hardly did she get as far as midriver when she returned to the quay, with a man in the bows showing the bridge how close they were to us by holding up the appropriate number of fingers. Having dropped off one man, they left again and gave the impression that someone had changed their mind and decided not to travel.

Shortly after this the big tug in front of us also decided it was time to go, and the lack of her presence in front of us providing a shield from the full force of the current whipped up by the wind, was a very noticeable change. It had been like Euston Station. Why so many boats chose to move off in the night we found difficult to understand. However, return to bed we did and Anto moved into the main lounge so as to act as watchkeeper and hear anything untoward happening.

The next day the weather was just as bad – really high waves and negligible visibility, which confirmed that the right decision was to stay put and wait until the wind abated and hopefully we would be able to see again. By 13.00 the wind seemed to have gone down a little and it was sufficiently clear to see the other side of the river, but by 14.30 the mist and rain came again. A short stroll into the town confirmed that we were not missing anything. It provided an opportunity to buy fresh bread however. We had a breadmaker on board in anticipation of the fact that we might find ourselves in places where it was not be possible to buy bread, but so far we had not needed to use it.

The next day the weather was fine by comparison to the previous 12 hours; it was a most welcome sight. Having woken early at 06.30, and after a quick cup of tea, we set off to the police to deal with the formalities of checking out of Serbia. The police station was busy with more staff than previously. There was a crew member from another ship, with a T-shirt showing its name, and another guy with a pile of at least 20 passports, and I thought that as I had already arrived I might be first, but there always seems to be so much conversation to deal with what appears a simple formality. However, the guy with the T-shirt was soon dealt with. I managed to get in before the other guy with the big pile of passports but was bitterly disappointed when I was told to go back to the ship and wait for the officers to come. "How long?" I asked. "Oh, five minutes," was the reply. So I did as I was bidden, but one hour later no one had come. Much activity had again started, with coal barges coming and tying up to the quay within a foot of us. Officers were coming to visit them but not us. After waiting a further half-hour I ventured back to the office in case they had forgotten us. Very timidly I presented myself but was again told to wait on the ship – somebody would come in about 10 minutes.

So back I went and after a further half-hour a very young and attractive blonde policewoman, together with a young customs officer who looked extremely pleased to have the good fortune to be accompanying her, arrived and when invited aboard politely asked if they could go inside. We gladly welcomed them. They examined the passports but did not wish to make any further examinations. When asked to sign off the form with which we could recover our ship's papers from the port captain, they made it clear that I had to go back to the office to have this done. So back I went, where they explained that I must have it signed off by the customs officer on the other side of the corridor.

I presented myself at the appropriate window. A gaunt and rather unpleasant man was busy writing in a big ledger, signing and stamping wads of forms and shuffling them about, stapling them together for the apparent benefit of a guy in civvies standing to his left. It was clear that he could not attend to me until this task was complete, the principle being to do only one thing at a time. I hoped that he still knew I was waiting. Eventually he appeared to have completed his lengthy task and turned to open his window with an air of 'what do you want?' I pushed though the aperture my piece of paper, indicating I needed it stamped, and by using hand gestures tried to indicate that his staff had been to our boat. Without any effort to confirm this he produced a little stamp with which he stamped the form, no signature being made, and stuffed it back at me.

Good, I thought, some progress. The policeman, having seen me waiting so long, had called me back to his window and signed the form, which I think may not have been normal procedure in that the customs should have stamped it before they signed off, so I returned to his window, double-checked and thanked him. I now had the authenticated form to take to the port captain to get our ship's documents returned and we would be able to leave

Serbia.

I had already noticed, whilst waiting on the boat for the inordinate length of time, that other people going from their ships to the group of offices were always carrying plastic bags, and maybe I was mistaken, but it seemed that on their return the bags looked lighter. So I had equipped myself accordingly this time and placed in the attaché case in which I keep all the important papers a plastic bag containing a bottle of whisky. I think I may have been wise. When I entered the port captain's office the guy I had seen on arrival, who had been very friendly and informal, was not there but instead two others were. By the amount of gold on their epaulettes they were clearly high-ranking. The more senior one took command and enquired of my needs. I showed him my fully signed-off dockets and pointed to our ship's papers which were on the desk, and explained to the best of my ability that we now wished to leave. He shuffled the various papers about to no apparent purpose. I explained that we had arrived at Mosács, stopped at Novi Sad and Belgrade, and were now here at Veliko Gradište and wished to leave for Romania. He put his hands together with his fingers touching and his elbows on the desk with an air of a counsellor and gave the impression that he was in no hurry. He then pointed to one of our Christian names – it could have been anything – and said, "What is this name?" I explained, "David," and thought that if we went through everybody's name like this we would be here all day. "Ah," he said, "please sit down and make yourself comfortable." Gosh, I thought, how long is this to take? But it gave me an opportunity because I had by now removed from the attaché case the plastic bag which I had folded in such a way that it was obvious that it contained a bottle. When I sat down some way from his desk I particularly made a point of leaving the plastic bag on the desk.

This may have done the trick because quite soon he brought the papers together and presented them to me, for which I thanked him and asked, looking at the plastic bag, was it in order to give them a present? The response in Serbian or Romanian or Hungarian appeared to be, "But of course". The other senior officer returned to the room – the timing seemed too coincidental in that it occurred immediately after I had surrendered the much-expected gift. I was able to include him in my warm expression of thanks and said how kind everybody had been and how much we had enjoyed Serbia.

To which he said, "Fine, perhaps we see you again." My facial expression may have betrayed my feelings, which implied it would be a long time before I would have reason to come back, so he said, "Maybe in England".

CHAPTER 10

RIVER DANUBE

THROUGH ROMANIA AND BULGARIA

THERE WERE TWO very interesting features we passed on this stretch of the river between Veliko Gradište and Orsova. The steep cliffs on both sides form the Gorge of Kazan; on the Romanian side at 967 are gigantic sculptures of faces in the granite cliffs which had been made by, we understood, Henry Moore.

A little further on at point 964 on the Serbian side was Trajan's Tablet; this was set in the cliff face, and a small tablet records the achievement of Trajan but only part of the original inscription is left. The original apparently referred to the opening of this route in 103 AD before the flooding of the gorge to construct the navigable route at a point lower down, but the tablet had been moved to its present position. Watchtowers were positioned all along both sides of the river; a most scenic stretch but their presence had an intimidating effect.

We arrived at Orsova (959) some seven hours after leaving Veliko Gradište, having crossed the border into Romania at Smederevo, and this was therefore our first stop in Romania. It was at a large basin in the river giving the effect of a lake. It has been formed as the result of a dam being built. The old town of

Orsova, which had stood on the bank of the river, is now submerged on the bed of this bay, a new town having been built on the edge of the new large lake in the river.

The river chart indicated where the harbour master's office was located, so it was not necessary to circle the bay, and we went straight to the right area. We were able to tie up at a quay alongside a working railway siding, which provided useful bollards. Much care was necessary when getting on and off the boat, to check that no trains were shunting up and down at the time, otherwise we would be down one crew member. A couple of railway workers helped us to make fast and I expressed our thanks with five Euros, not having yet acquired any Romanian currency. It was accepted with such grateful thanks one would have thought we had given them much more. As in Serbia we found that euros were generally accepted as legal tender even though at that time Serbia was not in the EU.

Again our first task was to walk the short distance to the official offices, which we had now found was referred to as 'Revision'. It was a large building into which we eventually found our way, having tried many locked doors and finding no sign of life. Trying each door in turn we were successful eventually and introduced ourselves to a burly uniformed Romanian. He seemed to understand and he enquired as to where our boat was. Because we were not able to stay there for the night we had not tied up at their quay. Subsequently we found out that we would have had to pay, whereas it was free where we were against the wall by the railway track, but exposed to the risk of the trains. When we pointed the boat out to him, he could just see it by leaning out of his window, and he was happy. He took us back downstairs to the police in an office we had missed. Here a not very friendly policeman took our passports, and having given him a list of our names we were told to wait outside five minutes.

We sat outside for 10 minutes and then gingerly tapped on his door. He was surprised on opening it to see us. He then made it clear that he meant us to wait on the boat. So off we went and half an hour later they arrived in force, four of them, the two we had already met plus two more. Very pleasantly they came aboard and we all shook hands. We offered them whisky which they gladly accepted, except the one who was able to speak perfect English – he appeared to be the spokesperson and had come along to see the ship and practise his English, which he had learned when visiting Cardiff. He explained how he had improved it by watching American movies, hence a slight American accent. The documentation was completed – not as extensive as when entering Serbia but requiring the application of the ship's stamp, which again was one of the items we had seen the wisdom of having made specially.

Everybody was very pleasant and we had to collect the ship's papers from the port captain before we left in the morning. The only advice before they left us was "Don't leave the ship unattended at any time". We had not planned to although we were aware that we would need another shopping visit soon. The problem we had with the battery charger had meant that a lot of our meat stock had been ruined, and whereas we had been able to buy a plentiful supply of fresh vegetables and fruit, other items were in short supply. Our brief stroll into the town in the late afternoon, when the rain had abated a little, produced eggs from a third of six grocery shops visited.

Sitting on the aft deck looking over to the bay at the lights of Orsova, with the light of the moon shimmering on the water, provided a tranquil scene as we relaxed, having eaten onboard a meal of tinned pilchards and many vegetables. We were fast eating into our reserve food stock but we felt comfortable, the wine stock was holding up and we felt fine; still a little apprehensive of what might happen, but at least we had got this far.

CHAPTER 11

RIVER DANUBE

– ORSOVA TO OLTENIȚA AND CONSTANTA

LEAVING ORSOVA AT 08.30 we soon arrived at the first of the only two locks on this section of the Danube, known as the Iron Gates Dam (949). The lock on one side of the river is owned by Romania and the lock on the other side by Serbia, but it was customary to have only one lock operating at a time. Today the Romanians were operating theirs and we passed through smoothly with little delay. It was a mammoth lock, with two chambers one after the other. Sixteen turbines produced electricity for Serbia and Romania. This section of the voyage provided the most spectacular scenery along the entire journey since Austria. The gorge sometimes reduced to only 20 metres wide and we were shocked to record a depth at one point of 80 metres.

Shortly after leaving the lock we arrived at Turnu Severin (930) and had no problems in being allowed to use a pontoon for an overnight stay next to the Revision Pontoon. Turnu Severin proved to be one of the most delightful stopping places on our voyage. We experienced very few difficulties in completing the official documentation procedures on arrival. Our walk into town provided us with the opportunity to equip ourselves with

Romanian currency. We now could feel more confident about our presence in the country, and we could spend money.

We had had an easy day, having organised a short leg to allow for any delay at the lock. The town was a pleasant place with an air of modern design intermingled with the old buildings; a pleasantly shaded park provided solace for the old to sit in the shade and the young to burn off their energy. A particular feature was the modern water feature, which mesmerised you as you were hooked onto watching the varied sequences of water displays.

A hotel near the river and the park provided a perfect opportunity to eat out at minimal cost. A simple but pleasant meal with wine on the outdoor terrace of a 1960s' style hotel was luxury to us. I was getting concerned about our fuel stocks – the gauge did not appear to have fallen much over the past few days, which concerned me that it may have stuck, in which case we were being misled as to the true position. My calculations indicated that we must be much lower than it would appear from the gauge, so refuelling was becoming a high priority.

The next morning, before taking our leave from the port captain, which was by comparison to earlier formalities a much easier exercise, I asked about fuel and was told there was a diesel barge moored some 50 metres back up the river, owned by a Mr Couach, who would be able to help us. So our first task that day was for us to pay him a visit. It was not too difficult to locate and tied up alongside a very large barge.

I made my way to the accommodation section at the stern, where two non-English-speaking chargehands were making early morning tea. I enquired for Mr Couach, but they said he was not available. Clearly I had to persist. I enquired when he would be available. I came to the conclusion he was not yet up, so I said

I was happy to wait. About an hour later a rather large bleary-eyed man appeared, who I assumed was Mr Couach. He led me to believe he might be able to help, but first I would have to wait. This I did whilst Mr Couach had his breakfast, showered, shaved and completed numerous other tasks, and eventually was ready to sell us some diesel fuel.

One might be forgiven for thinking that this would be a comparatively simple exercise, but no, first we had to drive to his office to complete the documentation and then we had to take the papers to the customs office and have them authenticated. Eventually we returned to the boat for what again one would normally assume would be a straightforward task. But no, the delivery pipes' nozzles were far too big to fit into the fuel inlets in the boat. They were only of use in fuelling huge tugs. Well, having got this far and being aware of the essential need for us to take on fuel, we could not afford to give up. The two deck hands searched high and low to see what they could find to overcome the problem. Many ideas were considered and various methods for delivery were tried but without success. No way.

Eventually a 50-gallon oil drum was obtained, and by use of a hand pump it was filled from the main supply. The oil drum was then positioned as near as possible to the fuel inlet, and believe it or not, the method of getting the fuel from the oil drum was going to be by siphoning. Now, those of us who have ever had to try this know that the only way to get the liquid to start to flow is by sucking it up the pipe and hopefully moving one's mouth from the end of the tube just before the liquid arrives there. You cannot stop sucking too soon, otherwise the liquid flows back. It is a matter of split-second timing and the consequence of getting it wrong is a mouth full of diesel fuel.

Fifty gallons meant filling and siphoning out the oil drum 10 times, and I hate to think about how many times the charge-hands tasted diesel fuel.

Eventually the task was completed and the favour I had promised to Mr Couach to get him to sell us fuel now had to be performed. But beforehand I was anxious to express my gratitude to the two chargehands who had performed such a momentous task and a tip was the least I could offer. But to my extreme surprise both refused to accept. They considered that they had just done their job. But they had done more than one would normally expect, surely. I pleaded with Mr Couach to persuade them to accept and give the money to their wives or their children if that helped them. He explained that tipping was not normal practice. But it was not normal to be drinking diesel fuel, I suggested. Eventually, with considerable reluctance, they took the money and at least I felt a little better for the considerable distaste they must have experienced. The favour to Mr Couach was to take him out in the boat and let him take a turn at the wheel, and of course have his photograph taken. It was the least we could do and it was a jolly little party – everybody had something to be pleased about.

By now it was well into the afternoon and the chance of getting to our next stopping place at Calafat, some 136 kilometres further on, was out of the question. So the only alternative was to return to our helpful stopping place of the night before at Turnu Severin, where we knew we would receive a warm welcome and there should be no problem. We were very happy to spend another night there and enjoy another visit into the town. The next day, having bid our friendly port captain farewell for the second time, we set off for Calafat at 06.30 and at 10.50 arrived at the second lock (864). This time it was the Serbian lock in use and again little delay was experienced; in fact we stopped well short of the lock gates, waiting for the signal to proceed. An official walked the 500 metres to us to check our papers and in a most helpful and polite manner gave us the all-clear to proceed. This was to be the last lock until we got to the Black Sea canal; so far we had passed through a total of 90 locks since leaving Sneek in Holland. After leaving the lock, the right bank of the river now became Bulgaria instead of Serbia, with Romania still on the left bank. We still had one more stop in Romania at Calafat. The land on either side of the river now flattened out; we were leaving the area of the great gorges which had proved so perfect a location for the Iron Gates locks to be built back in 1979.

The river now commenced to twist and wind through islands overgrown with vegetation but sometimes with white sandy beaches. The border town for checking into Bulgaria was Vidin (790), and having left Calafat at 10.30 we arrived there after an hour and a half. A further one and half hours later we were on our way again. It was a very big modern frontier post and efficient.

The buoys on the Danube had not been as easy to spot nor as frequent as one would have liked, but now they had shrunk to just being little cubes and even less frequent. Sometimes the route was very hard to follow. On one occasion we took a different route round an island than the river plan indicated because the buoys indicated differently and it gave us anxieties about going aground.

We arrived at Lom (744) at 15.00. There was a selection of stages to tie up to. At first selecting the wrong one, then safely secured at the right one, it proved to be the local youths' diving platform. We had no real reason to go into the town, except that we were concerned that we needed Bulgarian currency, so before we set off the next day we intended to make a quick visit in the hope of finding a bank.

As we walked from the boat we got into conversation with a young lady who was pleasant and friendly and helped in directing us. She said hello to a passing friend of hers who just happened to be a policeman. He asked to see our passports, which he examined with great enthusiasm but could find no trace of a Bulgarian visa stamp. We explained that we had entered Bulgaria at Vidin and had completed the formalities correctly.

On reflection we remembered that our passports had been taken away and then returned to us, so we had not actually seen them stamped and had not thought to look and check. So perhaps they had overlooked stamping them – not our fault, but how to explain to this difficult man? He ordered us back to the boat to stay there and not to leave under any circumstances. We complied with haste and a little concerned. We felt imprisoned on our own boat, under curfew, and after a time we decided to examine our passports very carefully. Bearing in mind that they all had numerous stamps in no particular order, they needed careful scrutiny. But sure enough, in each one, albeit in quite light ink, was the Bulgarian passport stamp at Vidin, which this stupid policeman had not spotted. Eventually, after two hours the delegation arrived, the policeman, his superior, a local solicitor and an interpreter who we later ascertained had been specially hired for this occasion. Our problem was not to appear to be clever dicks and embarrass the policeman in front of his superiors to such an extent that he might resort to retaliatory action and find something else to cause us a problem. They scrutinised the passports again and this time to their and our pretended surprise they found the stamp and all was forgiven. We said to hell with the bank and set off as soon as they had gone, a few hours later than we had intended. Our research indicated that Lom had been built on the site of the Roman garrison town of Almus. We had not had the opportunity to find out whether it was or not evident. Our delayed start meant we arrived at Somovit (608) later than we had planned. It had nothing to write home about.

The river had spread out and was much wider, and numerous islands created problems as to which side to pass on. When there was another boat travelling in the same direction it was much easier, as it was just a matter of following the route they took.

It was at 568 that disaster nearly occurred; perhaps I had not referred carefully to my notes, which would have warned me. Not many books have been written on cruising the Danube but one for essential reading is Bill and Laurel Cooper's *Back Door to Byzantium*, which is their account of the trip they made in 1995, and the first I am aware of since Les Horn's *Through Europe at Four Knots*, an account of his family's voyage in a small sailing boat. (There is of course *The Danube*, a river guide by Rod Heikell.) It was at this specific point that the Coopers went aground and had the devil's own job getting off, proving that this was a very difficult section. Clearly the helmsman, who was Neil at the time, had missed a buoy, which as it turned out was not surprising, since it involved a virtually 90-degree turn. But this again would have been expected if we had read our notes since the Coopers specifically refer to this odd route of the channel crossing almost at right angles across the river. Neil suddenly yelled that the depth had dropped to one metre, and this required the same action as pulling the communication cord on a train to give an immediate slowdown. Clearly we were in the wrong part of the river and the only course of action was to retrace our steps, turning the boat round in the smallest circle possible. I slowly edged back up the river, watching the depth finder and praying for it to slowly creep up to an acceptable and comfortable position. Taking ourselves back to the last buoy we had seen, we could then reconsider our position. By scanning the river with strong binoculars, we spotted on the extreme right, only a few metres from the bank, a red and a green buoy, indicating that the channel was there. The river was about 300 metres wide and the channel had moved from being slightly to the left to hard up to the right bank in a matter of 20 metres. No wonder we had nearly gone aground, and what we would have done I cannot imagine. There were very few other passing ships.

Needless to say, when we arrived at Rousse (495) some five hours later, having continued to follow a most tortuous route, we were much relieved. Rousse was straightforward with regard to the official procedures, the revision stage was easy to locate and the formalities comparatively simple to complete, or maybe we were just relieved that they were not taking the hours that they had previously taken.

We were directed for overnight mooring to a boat club in a harbour inlet, which was fine except that the space they made available for us required reversing into a space only two or three centimetres wider than the boat, but we were made most welcome and it was a safe refuge after a couple of taxing days. So we decided we would stay two nights and take the opportunity to see and enjoy Rousse.

The clubhouse was sparse by current UK standards but we were made very welcome, and the Commodore arranged for a girlfriend of his to be an English-speaking guide to show us around initially so that we could establish our bearings. In return for this favour we were expected to produce an entry in their club logbook for posterity.

Seeing the high standard of a previous Dutch entry some two months before us, we felt we had to produce something of equal note, and together with a photograph of our boat gave a brief resumé of our trip so far. Rousse at 495 is the fourth largest town in Bulgaria and the largest Bulgarian harbour on the Danube, which does not mean a great deal now with little traffic on the Danube, but in Roman times it was the base for their fleet of 60 ships.

The town was a delightful place full of neo-baroque 19th century buildings, with the central square and main street closed off as pedestrian precincts. In the evening the locals were all out for a stroll and it was colourful and relaxed. We had no difficulty in finding suitable restaurants for our two evenings out and the walk back to the boat on each occasion was without incident. We felt confident that we could leave the boat in a locked secure compound.

As previously explained, working out stopping places was important. Selecting places where there were likely to be facilities to tie up and be far enough on so that it would be possible to reach another suitable berthing place the following night was a prime consideration. We had enjoyed our two-night stay in Rousse and the berth in their little yacht club, although it was extremely tight to get into. It had been ideal; it had given us the opportunity to enjoy Rousse so much that we all felt it would be a nice place to return to some time.

Shortly after leaving Rousse we passed under the Friendship Bridge, the longest bridge across the Danube (7,340 ft). Built in 1954, this box-girder bridge is the only one linking Bulgaria and

Romania. The top part carries road traffic and the bottom part a railway line. Checking out of Bulgaria back into Romania for the section of our voyage through the Constanta Canal into the Black Sea was going to be necessary at Cernavodă, a distance of about 200 kilometres from Rousse. Clearly that was too far in one day and an interim overnight mooring place had to be selected.

It was clear that at Oltenița there were pontoons and the distance of 70 kilometres would leave a good 130 kilometres for the next day to Cernavodă, at which we could check into Romania again. This was our plan. As we approached Oltenița we noticed a couple of other boats close to us at times, but we did not pay much attention to them. We came alongside the pontoon and were helped with the tying-up by a young man who immediately required a payment. Nothing strange in that. Following the directions given, I went off on my own with all the papers again to deal with what I assumed would be quite routine. The port captain's office was in a house approached through a garden gate and along a path with carefully tended vegetable plants on either side. Knocking at the front of what could have been a cottage in any rural part of England, I waited timidly for it to be opened. A rotund motherly figure opened the door and to my enquiry for the captain made it clear to me that he was not there but was expected back soon, and she shepherded me into a room to wait for him.

This friendly and homely atmosphere relaxed me and I patiently waited, completely unaware of the reception I was shortly to be subjected to. I saw the captain return, coming up the path, middle-aged but looking young and fit and proud of his little neat homestead. He invited me into another room, which was obviously his office, and after a formal handshake invited me to sit down opposite him at his desk. I did not need to explain to him the purpose of my visit. It transpired that he had observed us and had been in one of the boats we had seen and had been shadowing us for sometime. Whether we could stay or not was a matter still to be dealt with. There were, he considered, much more important matters to be dealt with. I should explain he could speak English very fluently, and this was for him an opportunity to practise the language which he was not going to miss.

First, he announced, was the matter of the boat name; this was only displayed on the stern and international regulations required that it should also be displayed on each side of the vessel. This, I must admit, I was aware of and we had the letters ready to transfer on for this purpose, but I had decided at the last minute that they would look nicer if they could be first mounted on a nicely stained piece of wood which in turn could be affixed to the sides of the top cockpit rather than directly onto the side. I had as yet not found suitable pieces of wood for this purpose. And another thing, he went on to say in a manner that would not have surprised me if he had gone on to say that the was Herr Flick of the Gestapo, was that also under international regulations for ships in foreign countries we were correct in flying the flag of his country as a courtesy flag on the starboard side of our mast, but the requirements are that this should be the highest flag on the ship. Yet our own country's flag on the aft mast was higher. "Why do you insult my country so?" The flag we flew on the stern was a defaced blue ensign which we had as members of a club called the Cruising Club. It was a large flag and required a not insignificant flagpole. Our mast was not very high, sufficient to get satisfactory reception for the GPS mounted on the crossbars and designed with the problems of clearance for bridges etc. in mind. To further facilitate this it was possible to lower the top half.

Given these facts, from the angle of a small boat looking towards us, it might look as if our blue ensign at the stern was higher than the Bulgarian courtesy flag. I was certainly not going to argue the point. In making these points he had referred to international regulations on a number of occasions and sounded very much a barrack-room lawyer.

"As for whether you can stay overnight is dependent upon whether you get customs clearance. There is no customs post here on the river. There is a post in the town and we would have to get somebody to come from there. I do not have the authority to arrange that but I will make a request," he went on to say. "You can wait." Well, we had no choice and I suggested that I return to the boat to rectify in great haste the serious breaches of international regulations that we very much regretted we were in breach of.

I hurried back and together with Anto and Neil worked out what do. We took the two sets of letters and with a backing of white paper taped the name on the cockpit windows on each side of the boat. Using the extending boathook we lashed it to the mast to provide an extension on which we could fly the Bulgarian flag at a height which we hoped would satisfy our gauleiter and hopefully could be seen from his office window some distance away. It could now be seen how flags had been an important consideration prior to our setting off on the voyage, particularly this second half. As we checked in and out of each country we had to hoist a new courtesy flag, and it was obviously essential to have these ready for this purpose. It was no good waiting until you got to the border in the hope that you would be able to find some convenient place to buy them.

Obtaining flags for the countries in the first part of the voyage had been quite easy – they were quite common and stocked by many ship's chandlers, but as for Serbia, Romania and Bulgaria, the demand was not sufficient for them to be stocked. In plenty of time I had placed an order with the most well-known chandler in London and been assured that these would be available for me well before our planned return to the boat for the second half of our voyage, which would include these countries.

Well, although I had been chasing them they had advised me one week before we were due to leave that due to the heavy demand for flags for the celebration of the Queen's Golden Jubilee their suppliers would not be able to complete my order in time for us. They had had two months to make me aware of this problem. This created a concern, but I recalled that years ago I had known a girl who worked for a company in Liverpool called Flags, and I wondered if they still existed. Very quickly I established that they were now known as Ensign Flag Company, and off I went to see them.

"No problem, sir, you can have them for four o'clock tomorrow."

Sure enough they were made and delivered in less than 24 hours, and just two days prior to our departure we had a complete set of the flags we would need.

I did not need to return to the port captain's house-cum-office; he came to see us. Fortunately the matters of the name and flag were now in accordance with regulations, but he was less concerned about that. He regretted he had bad news. He had not as yet been able to get the necessary customs officials to agree to visit the port and clear us, which would create problems, but he was still working on it and was accompanied by his clerical assistant who was sending the necessary communications by fax under his dictation. It transpired that telephoning was not authorised.

He promised to return again shortly. Well he did, after an hour, with more disappointing news: replies had been received refusing, so this would mean we could not stay. We had by now, I should add, negotiated and agreed the fee for mooring overnight on this official pontoon with the man that had helped us to tie up, which we were not certain was in accordance with regulations but the amount we had been forced to agree to and the handing over of a bottle of whisky made us of the view that it was not. But at least we had got over this part of the berthing problems. Now we had still to be allowed by the government. We considered the alternatives. It would be impossible to get to Cernavodă, a distance of 129 kilometres, before darkness; it would take eight hours minimum and the question of travelling at night given our experiences so far was out of the question. The only solution would be for us to moor in the river near the bank, out of the way of any passing ships. We would need to take it in turns to do anchor watch since there could be dragging, and no, we would not be allowed to have a safety line secured to the pontoon. My negotiation and persuasion skills were to be stretched. Could they please request again and explain the importance of our position and the need for us to moor? We would be quite prepared to stay aboard and not go ashore. They could still only fax and again the response when eventually received was no. We were lucky that this port captain could speak good English, and by now his attitude had changed and he kept saying he was trying to help us and was doing all in his power to help, but it was the system. We had to believe he was sincere, but in the light of my initial experience with him I could not be certain.

"Well, could I speak with the people who make these decisions?" I asked. "We cannot telephone," he explained. "But do we know who they are and do we have the telephone number of the person who can decide?" "Yes, the Minister is in Bucharest." Well, using my own cellphone and on a rather expensive call routed from Bulgaria to England and back to Bucharest, I eventually, after much perseverance and with the port captain, his communications clerk, Anto, Neil and the pontoon man surrounding me, spent 20 minutes explaining to this Minister the position. Namely that I was a travel agent visiting his country to promote it to potential visitors. I was doing this journey down the River Danube with a view to writing a book, and if he did not grant me the necessary permission to moor overnight here in Oltenița I would be in serious difficulties and my account of this experience would have the effect of discouraging any of my fellow countrymen from ever visiting his beautiful country. I am pleased that eventually he agreed and said he would arrange for an appropriate fax to be sent to the port captain. What a relief and what a change in the port captain from the initial meeting. He had caused a lot of worry, but in the end had proved as helpful as the regulations permitted. After our experience at Oltenița we became very anxious to complete our voyage down the Danube and hoped that we might be able to get through without any similar experiences.

We had one more stop planned at Cernavodă (430) before we reached the canal, which would take us to Constanta on the Black Sea. We mounted double watch at all times to ensure that we missed none of the all-too-infrequent buoys marking the channel through a very flat part of the journey.

We arrived at Cernavodă, where we were to leave the River Danube for the canal to Constanta and the Black Sea. The distance of 129 kilometres took us nine hours and we were pleased that we had made it.

Immediately after another railway bridge, built in 1895 along the lines of the Forth Bridge in Scotland, we turned into the entrance to the canal on our right side. There were facilities for tying up overnight and we confirmed that we would be entitled to pass through the canal the next day. At what we thought we had arranged as the setting off time, we proceeded to untie and make our way to the entrance lock.

Work on the canal started in 1949 using slave labour in the form of minor criminals, critics of the party, peasants who rejected the collectivising project. Its construction was abandoned in 1953, by which time over 100,000 of the workers had died, earning the project the title of the 'Canal of Death'. President Ceauşescu resurrected the project in 1973, though the route was changed to a more easterly direction so that it emerges to the south of Constanta at Agigea.

As we approached it became evident that we had jumped the gun, and from a series of hand gestures in the absence of understanding of the language we got the message to return to the pontoon, tie up and wait until another boat came and then follow them into the lock. After a wait of about an hour a small cruise boat arrived and we followed her into the lock, the level of which moved very little. We endeavoured to keep up with the cruise ship, thinking this would be to our advantage at the other end, but we fell back. We were back in the less interesting but easier route of a canal, with no buoys or channel to worry about.

On either side the scenery emphasised the poorness of the country. It was very dreary, and horses and carts seem to be the form of transport. Periodically churches with their Eastern European architecture and children swimming in the canal broke up the monotony of this section. We passed a boy on a bicycle carrying a fishing rod at least 25 feet long – a feat of balance.

It was a dreary landscape but the 80 kilometres avoided a further 300 kilometres along the winding channel of the Danube to the delta and Sulina. We tried to keep up with the cruise boat, thinking that it would avoid any delay in getting through the lock at the end of the canal. Hopefully we would not have to wait for another boat. We failed to keep up, but when we arrived at the lock we could see our concern had not been necessary. The cruise boat was disembarking its passengers into coaches before the lock.

Our reception at the lock was very efficient, an official came aboard, checked our papers, gave us a map of the port and directed us to where we could tie up once through the lock.

The drop in the lock was only about a metre and a half and we were soon through into what was clearly a gigantic port. We made our way to where we understood we could tie up and found our way over scrubland and railways tracks to an office block where we found the port captain's office, paid $10 and confirmed that there was no problem in staying the night with a view to going on to Mangalia the next day.

We did not know whether we were in the right berth or not but at least we were tied up, surrounded by tugs and flies in a sea of overhead cranes.

We had arrived at the Black Sea. It was 22 June; we had left Budapest on 1 June. It had taken 22 days, a distance of 1,430 kilometres. We had travelled on 16 days, the other six days had been spent resting – four days in Novisad, one day in Rousse and of course one day had been taken up refuelling.

CHAPTER 12

THE BLACK SEA

– CONSTANTA TO THE BOSPHORUS

WE FELT THE weather was reasonable for us to commence the first leg of our voyage into the Black Sea. Having completed the checkout formalities with the Harbour Master we moved out of the dock area into the outer harbour and then out into the sea. It was a comparatively easy voyage, a distance of 23 nautical miles to Mangalia, still in Romania; the weather was fine and the sea state quite calm.

The mooring was not a problem and we had no difficulty in finding the Harbour Master's office and handed in our papers and passports, which were not stamped; this proved a problem the next day when we came to check out, the solution to which was that we had to make out again the form we had filled in on arrival with exactly the same detailed information. It was difficult to understand why we could not use the same form or take a copy, but no, that was not possible. We were able to do some shopping and to restock with fresh produce, and were then free to explore the town. It turned out to be a very pleasant seaside town, perhaps a little reminiscent of a North Wales holiday resort in the fifties. We found a very pleasant hotel, the President, situated right on the front, and despite it being 16.30 in the afternoon they were prepared to serve us with a full dinner in their large dining room in splendid isolation. After the attentive service and very enjoyable food and wine, refreshed we enjoyed a peaceful stroll along the seafront back to the boat.

After a restful day we were able to set off the next morning, leaving at 09.20 for Varna in Bulgaria, a distance of 53 miles, which took us a total of five hours. Again the sea was comparatively calm. As we approached the harbour we were repeatedly circled by a helicopter, which seemed to be trying to establish our creditability but made no contact with us on the VHF and eventually flew off and left us alone.

We managed to find a space at the end of the quay, which was popular with the locals to fish from. We had to disturb some of them to make way for our lines, but once this was overcome we had a good spot. Checking in and out was to prove most difficult; we wanted to leave the next morning at a reasonably early time to allow us sufficient time to get to our next port of call, which was to be Burgas.

We were required to pay a fee of US$50 for our overnight stay by way of port dues; the official requirement was that this had to be paid into a designated bank account, and the officially stamped paying-in counterfoil produced to the Harbour Master as evidence of payment before permission was granted to leave. The nearest bank was a thirty-minute taxi journey away and it did not open until 10.00 the next morning.

We wished to set off early, hopefully by 08.30, so a considerable amount of effort was going to be required to overcome this bureaucratic problem, all of this being made difficult by the fact that none of the officials spoke proper English and we had gleaned all this in pidgin form.

We were told that there was a yacht club in the port and the Commodore might be able to help us. We located an area comprising a group of sailing boats, which could possibly have a collective association about it and a bit of a clubhouse, but it was very far removed from the vision of a British yacht club with the usually yachtee types. We approached anybody we found moving on or near any of the boats, enquiring as to who might be the Commodore, but all of them declined any responsibility for that position. We eventually found a member who could speak very good English and we were able to explain to him our plight.

He took us to one of the members who had previously been approached and had denied the responsibility or had not understood our question, who turned out to be the Commodore. Together with the English-speaking club member we all made our way to a workshop room under the clubhouse, filled with all manner of boat jumble which could have proved useful if we had been in need of any repairs. After an hour of long discussion, we managed to establish that the Commodore did have the authority to accept the money, on the understanding that he would pay it into the designated account, and the receipt he would provide on this basis was sufficient to satisfy the port authorities with regard to the payment. Why could we not have been made aware of this facility in the first five minutes of our discussions? The reason became clear when the question of the fee for performing this service was raised.

There was the cost of a taxi to be taken into account, the time involved, the responsibility, and not least the fact that he was the only person entrusted with the responsibility to do this, so his fee and expenses amounted to significantly more than the US$50 port dues themselves. But at least the problem was cracked and we could relax, knowing that weather permitting we could set off the next day without too much delay.

In fact the next day, having reported to the Harbour Master's office at 08.00, we received the delegation of his representative and the customs official to the boat quite quickly and we were able to be on our way by 08.30.

The voyage of 57 kilometres was not too bad, and again the sea quite smooth, so we arrived at Burgas at 15.30, still in Bulgaria. It was quite an industrial port but there was no difficulty in finding a place to tie up amongst the freighters and cargo ships, but a long wait ensued before we were able to obtain clearance to get off the boat.

Our experience had taught us by now not to break the rules, and we must be patient. We hoisted the Q flag and waited and waited, and just when our patience was about to run out they arrived in force. Having said goodbye to those three further officials, the port captain, the customs officer and the immigration police, I contemplated how many officials we had had to see on our journey since Budapest.

Whereas the section of our voyage from Sneek in Holland to Budapest had involved passing through a total of nearly 100 locks, on this part of our journey from Budapest it had been officials we had to pass, not locks. These three had been very pleasant and had arrived one and half hours after our arrival, which by comparison to many of our stops was a considerable improvement. Freedom was granted to visit the town, but with a strict warning about being careful with our possessions and not to mix with the gypsies.

We left the dock area through tight security-checking at the dock gates and found a very lively and bright town with numerous shops and hotels, one of which proved an ideal venue to return to that evening for dinner, after which, on the way back to the ship, we came to understand the reason for the warning about the gypsy women. As we took a shortcut through a small park we were accosted by a flock of heavily made-up females intent on offering all manner of sexual services and resorting to physically mauling each of us intimately to establish the seriousness of their offers. Sufficient to say we declined with a tirade of verbal abuse at them.

On the day we had intended to leave from Burgas to Igneada in Turkey, we got up at 06.00, but having climbed the eight floors to the Harbour Master's office, which provided a panoramic view over the quay and docks, we were presented with a very unfavourable weather forecast, and he strongly recommended we stay in port another day. So we aborted our planned departure and rested instead, enjoying a pleasant stroll and lunch in town and being careful on our return to the boat to take a different route than through the park.

It was now Thursday 27 June and we had plans to get to Istanbul by 30 June, so when this time, having climbed the eight floors to the Harbour Master's office, we were provided with a weather forecast which supposedly indicated it was going to be a calm day, we decided we should put in motion the procedure for our departure. This first involved paying the Harbour Master US$50; then we had to retrieve our passports from another office at the dock gates, but we were told that they would be brought to the boat, and sure enough after half an hour they came, complete with a customs official who required us to sign a declaration that we were carrying no cargo, and we were deemed free to go.

We set off at 08.30, the course having been plotted on the GPS for Igneada, our first port of call in Turkey. It soon became apparent that either the weather forecast was wrong or we had incorrectly interpreted it. The boat seemed to do everything but turn over, and the sea state could be described as most unpleasant. The need to try and keep the boat straight onto the big waves rather than have them catch us broadside, which made the boat roll, resulted in us going off course frequently and required periodic adjustment. Despite the rough sea we completed the 52 kilometres in just over seven hours, and much to my relief, steamed into the harbour at Igneada at 15.45. The only space for the tying-up of visitors' vessels was occupied by a Turkish Navy Coast Guard ship which appeared to be pre-World War II.

However, they were most helpful and beckoned us to come alongside and tie up to them. The duty officer was most pleasant and after referring the question to his captain, returned to say that it would be quite in order for us to stay there for half an hour. This would at least enable us to ferret out the Harbour Master, and hopefully complete the complicated but very necessary formalities for ships and people entering Turkey.

This involved obtaining visas, at a cost of £5, and the issue of a transit log for the boat; with this in mind we had made contact by email prior to our departure from the UK, advising him that this would be our first port of call in Turkey. It was not difficult to locate his house, set back from the port itself, and we were made most welcome and invited to join him in a beer. It was obvious that he had consumed quite a few that day already. As regards obtaining visas, and as for getting a transit log, this was out of the question so in a word he was a complete waste of time and we were in breach of the law by being in Turkey without stamped visas in our passports and proper documents for the boat.

We returned to the boat, where with the help of the navy we repositioned it alongside a moribund fishing boat on the end of the quay, just around the corner from our naval host ship. We had developed a problem with the port engine, which became apparent as we undertook this manoeuvre, which created further cause for concern. It transpired to be overheating, for which the cause was not apparent.

The Coast Guard vessel was filling with water from a tap in a small hut on the quay, so perhaps we could do the same, I thought. Enquiries from, by now, my friend the duty officer of the Coast Guard ship indicated that this was the Turkish Navy's own private supply, but after again referring my request to the higher authorities we were told that we could have 200 litres free when they had finished. In return for this favour I agreed that I would try and promote his brother's hotel with British tourists. A promise I regret I have as yet been unable to fulfil, although I did try and locate it when driving through his town some time later, but it was so far away from the centre I regret I gave up.

When the water-filling exercise was complete we walked into the village and found very little to tempt us to eat out that night, so returned to eat on board whilst the entire crew of the Coast Guard ship enjoyed a BBQ on shore, but we received no invitation to join the party.

Our experience with the weather, in that it had been so bad when we were told it was going to be good, made me most concerned, and when the weather forecast looked bad I decided it would be wiser to stay put for another day before setting off on our final, slightly longer, last leg on the Black Sea to Poyrac at the entrance to the Bosphorus, a distance of 75 kilometres. As it turned out it was a perfect day and the sea looked as calm as a millpond.

Anto and I took a taxi into the town, which was some distance from the port and certainly too far to walk, and left Neil in charge of the boat. We stocked up with plenty of fresh fruit and vegetables and treated ourselves to a delightful meal at a fish restaurant with a wonderful view over the sea; although every time we saw a policeman we quickly made tracks in the opposite direction in view of our illegal status. Eventually we managed to get a taxi back to the boat, which to our surprise proved difficult since it seemed to be a holiday for taxi drivers.

The Navy vessel left in what involved a considerable amount of effort by all the crew, both in getting the engines started and making way in a cloud of black smoke bellowing from the funnels. The sea was not calm but not as bad as the previous experience, and our route took us a long way out into the Black Sea to make the shortest distance for this leg.

CHAPTER 13

DOWN THE BOSPHORUS TO ISTANBUL

Eventually, after nine hours, the longest of any day at the wheel, I was more than glad that we had completed the Black Sea section and were now in the Bosphorus, even though this involved funnelling along with numerous large ships into this narrow waterway.

Poyrac was in a large cove on the opposite side of the Bosphorus, so we immediately had the difficult task of crossing the down and the up channels of the continuous line of very large ships. It was like crossing a busy road; we were all watching for a break in the traffic. It was difficult to estimate how fast the ships were moving, and bearing in mind the current, how much space we needed to get across without running the risk of being run down by a big tanker which might take a distance of a mile to stop. We made it by going straight across the minute we felt comfortable that there was a sufficient gap. The current had taken us off slightly so we came back up to the entrance to the harbour behind a long breakwater.

As we entered, the significance of the day became apparent. To say the least, it was packed; being a weekend, local boat owners from Istanbul had not surprisingly taken to the water for the weekend. What a perfect trip to go up the Bosphorus.

All sections of the quay were occupied and numerous boats anchored in the bay. It was difficult for us to find a place to anchor and be sure that we did not swing into other craft. The situation was made more difficult by the arrival at the same time of a 100-foot palace of a yacht. The crew, having anchored, took a line astern to the quay, a distance of 70 feet, to stop it swinging at night; I assume not to disturb the sleep of the wealthy owners. They did however have the consideration to suspend a fender from the middle of the rope to draw attention to its presence. In the dark it would have been a dangerous hazard to any unsuspecting vessel manoeuvring in that area.

We stayed onboard and ruled out any idea of using the dinghy to go ashore, mainly because we could not see a gap anywhere on the quay where we could get ashore, and secondly we would be illegal again. It was delightful weather and sitting on deck was most relaxing. We had got this far, but were still apprehensive about the next day and going down another M1 of shipping.

The final day of our voyage dawned for the grand finale: the sail down the Bosphorus and across the Golden Horn and past Istanbul, which was the equivalent of Piccadilly Circus. Large and small ferryboats mingled with big ships moving into and from the sea of Marmaris, as well as large cruise ships arriving and departing. Although it was not a long distance, we were going to need our wits about us.

Our anxieties were running high and the first problem for the day materialised as we raised the anchor. We found we had fouled a cable. The anchor had dragged a cable off the seabed and was pulling it up as it rose from the water. We were effectively hooked to it and the question was how to reach down and release it. Dropping the anchor down again did not have the required effect of dislodging the offending cable.

We had onboard an extending boathook, bought at Duisberg at the start of our journey up the Rhine; this had proved invaluable when negotiating the deep locks on the Rhine Main Canal when it was necessary to hook the ropes on and off the lock sides. An essential piece of equipment, which all boats should carry. So we realised that this would be useful in the reverse by way of reaching down instead of up. Anto lay over the bow as far as possible with the fully extended boathook, and with Neil holding his legs we brought the anchor high enough for him to reach the offending cable. He was then able to unhook the cable off the anchor. The cost was losing the extension half of the boathook, which came away under the pressure. Since we had no more locks to negotiate the loss was not devastating. We were freed.

Once clear of the harbour, all looking out again for a gap in the convoy of big ships coming up on our side, we had to cross to the opposite side. There appeared to be many more than the previous day, and it was some time before we made a dart at full speed across to the far side. Once in position we kept close in and as long as we maintained a good lookout behind as well as in front and kept our calm, we could enjoy looking on both sides as we passed the enchanting landscape, being careful to skirt the ferry-boats arriving and leaving the landing stages situated at each of the various towns on the bank.

Soon we came level with the splendid Ciragan Palace Hotel, operated by Kempinski Hotels; a converted palace, the splendour of the architecture was appreciated best from the river, the new section blending in perfectly with the old magnificent palace. It had been our intention to stop here and celebrate by dining in their famous restaurant, Tugra. Permission had been obtained from the police via the hotel for us to moor overnight at an extortionate cost for security. I was anxious about the port engine overheating and the possibility that this might create a problem in completing the last bit of our voyage, particularly since we would need all the power we had to manoeuvre at close quarters among the heavy traffic round the Horn. The possibility of having to do this with only one engine, should the port one fail to restart the next day, filled me with dread.

Bearing all this in mind I decided against the stopover and we sailed by giving them a polite hoot and a wave. We could easily go to the hotel from the marina for a visit when safely moored. It would not be quite the same without our boat moored outside but the chances of sleeping with the amount of turbulence in the water making all the boats bob around like corks would have been impossible. We now had to cruise along the coast, weaving our way between numerous ships at anchor.

As we approached the Golden Horn I was reminded that this was surely the only way to arrive in Istanbul, namely by sea. I recommend it to anybody contemplating a cruise: this is an essential port of call; Topkapi on the top of the cliffs, the Blue Mosque on a hill, with the outline of Santa Sofia behind it, along with the numerous minarets, and the Galata Tower in the foreground provide a spectacular sight.

The water was extremely choppy with the currents, and the continuous ferry-boats criss-crossing confirmed my expectations of Piccadilly Circus at sea. Eventually we reached the entrance to the Atakoy Marina, easily recognisable by the backdrop of the Crown Plaza Hotel which gave a useful landmark to make for. We were careful to watch for the fast hydrofoil ferry, which departs just by the entrance to the marina and shoots out like a boat out of hell. Before long we were in and at journey's end – what a relief.

A quick call on the VHF soon produced a marina tug to escort us to our berth, our intended arrival having been communicated to them and a berth booked. It all seemed easy except that after a journey requiring considerable concentration the final act required reversing the boat into a space with less than a foot spare on either side. The risk of damaging these expensive boats called for considerable care and the need to be sure to go straight as we backed in. Fortunately one of the marina tug men picked up the anchor buoy to which we would be secured at the bow. Whereas their assistance was much appreciated, the inexperience of this marina man, who held on to the line attached to the buoy so firmly, meant that without appreciating why, I could not get the boat to reverse back to the quay where other marina staff were waiting for lines to be thrown to them to make the boat secure. Tired and bewildered, I was revving the engines, thinking the depth of water was the problem and we were on a mound. All I was succeeding in doing was pulling from their sockets the arms of the guy who was holding on to the line connected to the buoy at the bow as though his life depended upon it. I hate to think of the consequences if he had let go at this point. We would have reversed into the quay with such force that the damage would have been tremendous.

Fortunately I had the presence of mind to stop everything and survey the situation to see what the problem was, and soon we were safely secure and ready for our celebratory drink at journey's end. A brief look into the engine room revealed not a pretty sight. The strain I had placed on the engine in the last five minutes had been the straw that had broken the back of the port engine, which had been showing signs of ill health for some time. Water was all over the place, and steam pouring out always gives a worse impression than it really is. But so what; we had arrived and that's what mattered. We had made it thanks to a lot of good luck and the tenacity of all the crew.

APPENDIX 1A

LOG – SNEEK TO SAAL

	HRS	LOCKS	KMS
SNEEK TO BERGUM	3,5	-	22
BERGUM TO DELFZIJL	8,5	2	98
DELFZIJL	-	-	-
DELFZIJL TO EMDEN	4,5	1	31
EMDEN TO HAREN	10	4	69
HAREN TO BEVERGERN	9,5	9	71
BEVERGERN TO HENRICHENBURG	10	1	93
HENRICHENBURG TO DUISBERG	8	5	50
DUISBERG	-	-	-
DUISBERG TO DUSSELDORF	5	-	42
DUSSELDORF TO KOLN	7	-	62
KOLN TO NEUWIED	9	-	82
NEUWIED TO BINGEN	3	-	30
BINGEN TO MAINZ	3	-	30
MAINZ TO HANAU	7	5	56
HANAU TO MILTENBERG	8,5	6	70
MILTENBERG TO LOHR	9,5	5	73
LOHR TO OCHSENFURT	9	7	72
OCHSENFURT TO SCAWEINFURT	7	7	62
SCAWEINFURT TO BAMBERG	4	52	
BAMBERG	-	-	-

BAMBERG TO NÜRNBERG	9	6	66
NÜRNBERG TO BELINGRIES	10	7	63
BELINGRIES TO SAAL	5	3	40
	158	**72**	**1284**

APPENDIX 1B

LOG – SAAL TO BUDAPEST

	HRS	LOCKS	KMS
SAAL TO REGENSBURG	3	2	30
REGENSBURG TO DEGGENDORF	6¼	2	94
DEGGENDORF TO PASSAU	4¼	2	59
PASSAU TO LINZ	7¾	3	92
LINZ TO YBBS	7½	3	76
YBBS TO KROMMS	5	1	60
KROMMS TO VIENNA	-	2	71
VIENNA	-	-	-
VIENNA	-	-	-
VIENNA TO BRATISLAVA	4	1	57
BRATISLAVA	-	-	-
BRATISLAVA TO ESZTERGOM	11	1	148
ESZTERGOM	-	-	-
ESZTERGOM TO BUDAPEST	4	-	67
	53	**17**	**754**

APPENDIX 1C

LOG – BUDAPEST TO ISTANBUL

	HRS	LOCKS	KMS
BUDAPEST TO DUNAFÖLDVÁR	5	-	90
DUNAFÖLDVÁR TO BAJA	5	-	83
BAJA TO APATIN	8½	-	77
APATIN TO NOVISAD	8½	-	143
NOVISAD	-	-	-
NOVISAD	-	-	-
NOVISAD	-	-	-
NOVISAD	-	-	-
NOVISAD TO BELGRADE	5½	-	91
BELGRADE TO VELIKO GRADIŠTE	7½	-	111
STORMBOUND IN VELIKO GRADIŠTE	-	-	-
VELIKO GRADISTE TO ORSOVA	7	-	96
ORSOVA TO TURNU SEVERIN	4	1	22
DAY REFUELLING	-	-	-
TURNU SEVERIN TO CALAFAT	7	2	136
CALAFAT TO LOM	5	-	52
LOM TO SOMOVIT	8¼	-	136
SOMOVIT TO ROUSSE	10	-	109
ROUSSE	-	-	-
ROUSSE TO OLTENIȚA	3¾	-	70
OLTENIȚA TO CERNAVODA	9	-	129

CERNAVODA TO CONSTANTA	6	2	84
CONSTANTA TO MANGALIA	3	-	23
MANGALIA TO VARNA	7	-	53
VARNA TO BURGAS	7	-	57
BURGAS	-	-	-
BURGAS TO IGNEADA	7½	-	52
IGNEADA TO POYRAC	9	-	75
POYRAC TO ISTANBUL	3½	-	23
	137	**5**	**1712**

APPENDIX 1D

SUMMARY

	DAYS	HOURS	LOCKS	KMS
SNEEK TO SAAL	24	158	72	1284
SAAL TO BUDAPEST	14	53	17	754
BUDAPEST TO ISTANBUL	29	137	5	1712
	67	**348**	**94**	**3750**

APPENDIX 2

YACHT HAVENS HOTELS & RESTAURANTS

YACHT HAVENS

HOLLAND

Sneek:	Brandsma Jachten Sneek Bedrijven terrein 't Ges Eeltje Baasweg 8 / 8606 KA Tel: 0515 – 425000 Fax: 0515 – 420505 http://www.brandsma-jachten.nl
Deflzijl:	Jachthaven 't Dok van m.b.v. "Abel Tasman" Aagesloten bij K.Z. & R.V. Neptunus, N.N.W.B Eemskanaal NZ 2, 9934 RG Delfzijl Tel: +31 (0)596 – 616560

GERMANY

Emden:	Emder Yacht-Club e. v. Postbach 1426 26723 Emden Tel: 04921 997147
Duisburg:	Ruhrorter Yacht Club Rheinkilometer 781, 1 R AM Eisenbahnbassin 42 4100 Duisburg 13 Tel: 0203 / 84209
Newiad:	Motor Yacht Club Neuwied e V Hafenmeister Rheinstr 180 56564 Neuwied Tel + Fax: 0 26 31 / 35 36 37 / 35 36 44
Bingen:	Motor-Yacht-Club Bingen ev Winterhafen 55411 Bingen am Rhein Tel: 067 21 / 12520
Mainz:	Dmyv AM Winterhafen 55131 Mainz Tel: 06131 / 23 20 30

Nurnberg: Herzlich Wilkommen
Motoryacht Club Nurnberg
Aischweg 40
90449 Nurnberg

AUSTRIA

Vienna: Marina Wien
Handelsgescllschaft M.B.H
A 1020 Wien Handelskai 343
Tel: +43 1 7260762
Fax: +43 1 726 0762 15
E-mail: office@marine-wien.at

BRATISLAVIA

MYSB (Motor Yacht Service Bratislava)
(Dunaj KM 1864,8)
Bazen 1V 5 Vicie Hrdlo 82107 Bratislava
Tel: +4217 240 9862

HUNGARY

Estergom:Leitner Tamas
Papp Attila
Nautica
2500 Esztergom
Bajcsy Zs U7
Tel: (33) 11 707
Fax: (33) 12 395

Budapest: Wiking Marina
H – 1033 Budapest
Hajogyari
S216ET117
Tel: (361) 388 6153
Fax: (361) 250 3950

SERBIA

Dunafoldvar: International Yacht club
c/o Karl Fehervary
Pentdeiut 5
H-720 Dunfloldvar
06.75 / 3417 29

Baja: Hotel & Campsite Sugovica
H 6501 Baja
Petofi S21Get PP32
Tel: (00 36) 79 /321 755)

TURKEY

Istanbul: Atakoy Marina
Sahil Yolu 34710
Atakoy, Istanbul
Turkey
Tel: (0212) 560 42 70
Fax: (0212) 560 72 70

HOTELS

Turnu Severin:	Park Continental 2 Carol 1 Blvd Turnu Severin Romania Tel: +40 52 312851 Fax: +40 52 316988 E-mail: parc@drobara.expertivo
Bourgas:	Hotel Bulgaria 21 Akexandrouska Str 8000 Bourgas Bulgaria Tel: +359 56 842 610 Fax: +359 56 841 291 E-mail: hotelbulgaria@zplus.bg
Mangalia:	Hotel President Str Teilor Nr. 6 8727 Mangalia Romania Tel: +40 41 7558 61 Fax: +40 41 7556 95 E-mail: office@hpresident.com

Rousse: Danube Hotel
5 Svoboda Square
7000 Rousse
Bulgaria
Tel: 082 8229 29
Fax: 082 8229 52

Miltenberg: Brauerai Keller
63897 Miltenberg
Germany
Tel: 09371 5080
Fax:

RESTAURANTS

Budapest Postakolsi Etterem
Budapest 111
Foter 2
Tel: 0250 2286
0453 2221

Gundels
Allatkerti ut 2
Budapest 1146
Tel: 00 36-1-468-4040

APPENDIX 3

MAP OF ROUTE

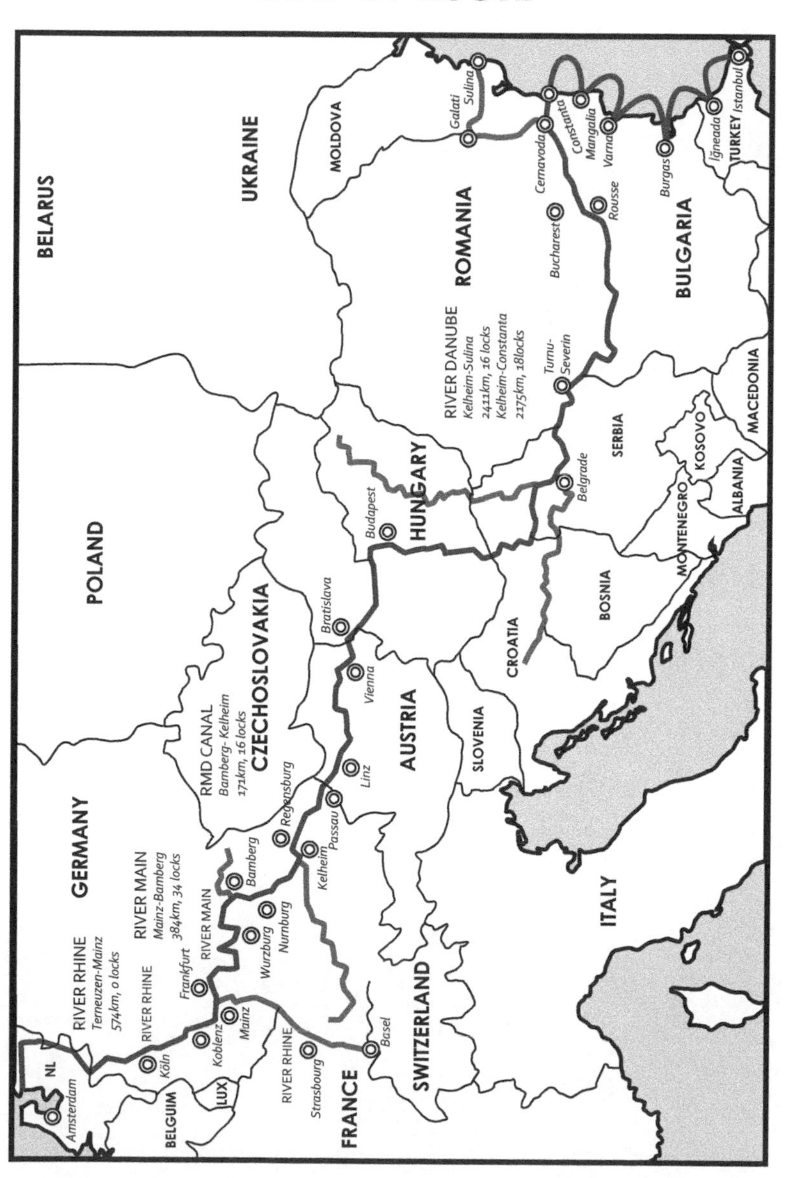

APPENDIX 4

THE BOSPHORUS

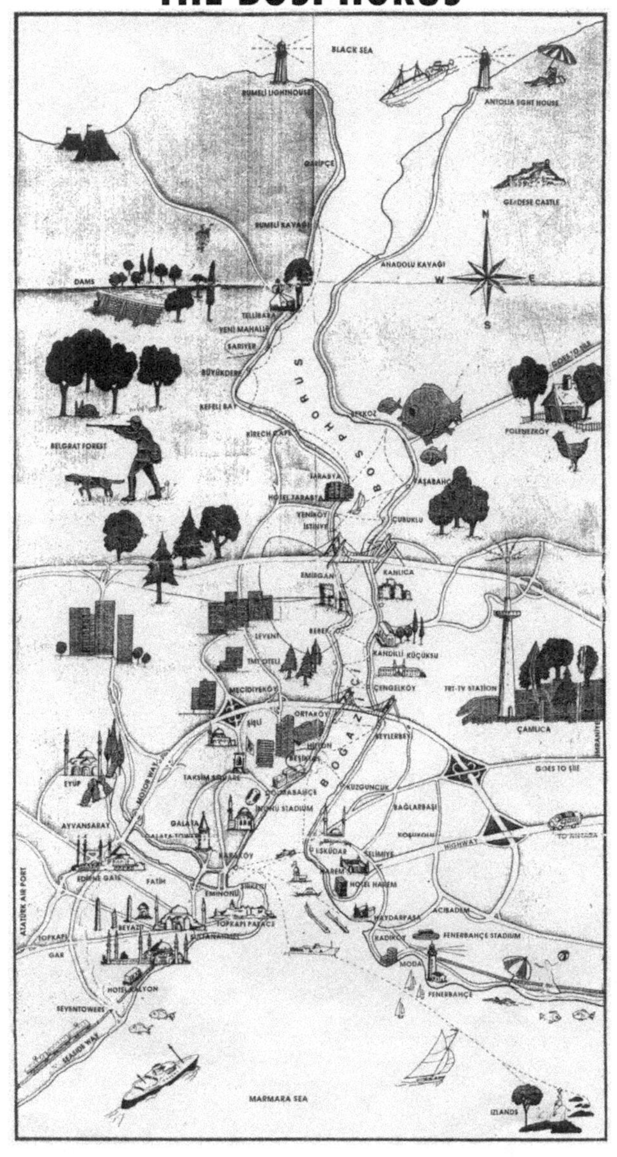